What to Do
When
The Shit Hits the Fan

Dave Black

Skyhorse Publishing

www.skyhorsepublishing.com

10 9 8 7 6 5 4 3 2 1

Library of Congress Cataloging-in-Publication Data

Black, David.
    What to do when the shit hits the fan/David Black.
        p. cm.
    Includes index.
    ISBN-13: 978-1-60239-133-8 (pbk. : alk. paper)
    ISBN-10: 1-60239-133-5 (pbk. : alk. paper)
    1. Survival skills. 2. Emergency management. 3. Safety education. 4. Disasters. 5. Terrorism. I. Title.

GF86.B53 2007
613.6'9—dc22   2007017219

Printed in the United States of America

Dedication

Every book I've seen on Emergency Preparedness in the last ten years has relied heavily on two main sources for their information: FEMA and the American Red Cross. In fact, many books are essentially word-for-word copies of FEMA and Red Cross materials, probably because they are the best source of comprehensive preparedness material. There are some inevitable similarities in portions of this text because the basic steps of preparedness and planning are unavoidably common to every agency or individual who provides preparedness information or training. Hopefully I've provided some additional unique information that will be both interesting and useful, and from a fresh and honest perspective.

It's impossible to write a book like this without dredging up a lot of memories, good and bad. I did a lot of thinking about old paramedic and firefighter partners. It's been years since I've seen any of them, but the respect I have for their bravery and skill is no less now than it was when I rode with them. I dedicate this book to them. I will also take this opportunity to thank the Red Cross for all the support they provided us on those long cold nights and blistering days when we were fighting fires or dealing with other tragedies.

Dave Black
Blanding, Utah, 2007

Contents

Chapter 3

Chapter 4

Chapter 5

Chapter 6

Chapter 7

Chapter 8

1.   The Author's Background

I'm a baby boomer. As a typical kid in that generation living in 1950s California, I learned through the paranoia of my parents and teachers that disaster and doom were just around the corner in the form of a giant earthquake or a nuclear holocaust. We trained in school to crawl under our desks, as though this move would save us while everyone else in southern California was being vaporized by the blast. My parents bought into the bomb shelter idea, and I remember sitting on the couch listening to traveling shelter salesmen present their doomsday routines. It was an odd time to be growing up. Communism was the greatest evil and would surely bring the world to a horrible end. My parents moved to Utah, partially to get away from the nuclear and earthquake threats, and partially because they were Mormons. Interestingly, one of my most vivid memories is of the Bear Lake earthquake in 1959, which left some cracks in our house. A second is of the Cuban missile crisis. The earthquake was interesting and even fun, but the Cuban crisis was the first time I can remember stark, stomach-wrenching fear. For a day and a night, we all thought our lives would be snuffed out and the world destroyed.

Through all of this there was one thing I took comfort in. The Church had for decades insisted that member families put together and maintain a two-year stockpile of food and essential supplies, and my parents complied. It was an inconvenience and seemed unnecessary at the time. My parents had experienced the Great Depression and knew the value of preparing for the worst, but I was part of the Pollyanna *Leave It to Beaver* generation that was unaffected by real disasters. In the end the two-year supply did provide some psychological comfort, and now that I've had fifty years to see the real world I realize it was exceedingly smart to have that sort of resource available.

When I graduated from high school in 1970 I did what good Mormon boys do. I went on a two-year mission. Mine was to Bolivia. During my time there I went through two revolutions and half a dozen riots. My apartment was dynamited, I was shot at, and old P-51 Mustang aircraft bombed and strafed our neighborhood. Worse than all that, my mission president's wife took a disliking to my rebellious attitude and haircut and I eventually found myself banished to work with the rural Quechua, one of the most mistreated, impoverished peoples in the Americas. Assignment to the Quechuas was supposed to be a punishment, and for nearly two years I lived in the Andes at 14,000 feet with no electricity, no running water, no heat, plastic on the windows of my thatched mud hut, and the countryside as my toilet. I ate the native diet and cooked on fires and gas stoves. Transportation was in the back of a truck or by burro. When I was hungry or cold I chewed coca leaves or drank coca tea. I learned to huddle beneath my poncho with a tiny candle to keep myself from freezing. I even delivered babies and removed bullets. I lived the austere Third World life that most spoiled Yankees have no sense of. In the end I distanced myself from the church and the city-based missionaries. I came to understand and thrive in the conditions the bigoted old president's wife had condemned me to. These were lessons that I will never forget, and they are the fundamental lessons that made me feel I could survive almost anything. My first week back in the States, a major winter storm snowed the town in and caused a three-day blackout. I took it in stride, warming myself with a candle under a poncho and cooking on an old alcohol camp stove. It was obvious that the effect a disaster has on an individual is relative to what a person is used to dealing with.

After some long years in the military in intelligence and special ops, I became a ski bum. Real ski bums are always broke, so to get a better handle on cash, I tested for a firefighter position and was soon hired on with a very busy fire department in Ogden, Utah. It was my second year with the department when an incident occurred that suddenly made me an "expert." Two boys and their dog were stranded on a steep cliff above the swollen Ogden River. One of the boys had fallen and was hanging on precariously, waiting for rescue. The fire department could not reach them from above, and the ladder truck had not been able to reach them from across the river. I was on my day off, in a hot tub, when the department called. To me, a climber of twenty years then, the rescue was easy and unspectacular. The next day, however, a picture of me dangling near the patient was on the front page of the *Chicago Tribune*. Within days I was fielding calls from fire and rescue agencies all over the country, asking for training. I rushed myself through paramedic school and by the end of the year I found myself carrying multiple pagers and radios to keep in contact with all the volunteer and

specialized rescue teams I was involved with. I was fighting
fires and seeing a thousand critically ill or injured patients
a year in the streets, dealing with the demons that burned
out paramedics deal with. It was too much to handle, and I
quit the fire department and disappeared into the rural west
to work with small EMS agencies. Later I graduated from
Weber State with a composite bachelors degree in Foreign
Languages, Emergency Care and Rescue, and Geology
and almost immediately found myself overseas building
EMS and community disaster response and management
systems in places like Saudi Arabia, the Balkans, and
the former Soviet Republics. With the exception of three
years at Weber State University as the administrator of
their external health sciences studies programs, and three
years as an emergency planner for the health department
in Utah, consulting has been my mainstay. There's nothing
more satisfying than learning that the training I have
provided was used successfully to save some lives. I've
had that amazing experience several times now, and I feel
lucky for having found myself in the position to provide
that training.

It's with this perspective that I bring you this book.

2.   The Nature of Disaster

What constitutes a disaster is relative to the event and the
effect it has on the individual or group. We, as Westerners in
the Northern Hemisphere, are spoiled and prosperous. Even
our poorest would be considered prosperous in the eyes of
poorer people like my Quechua friends. Our prosperous
lives and governments shield us from discomfort and
discontinuity. A drought in California just raises prices in

America. A drought in eastern Africa could kill millions. A disaster to a Quechua Indian would be an earthquake that crushes his mud hut, kills his children, and wipes out his village. A broken fingernail could be a "disaster" to a New England debutant.

A disaster is commonly defined as an event causing widespread destruction and distress. A grave misfortune. A crisis event that surpasses the ability of an individual, community, or society to control or recover from its consequences. For most North Americans a disaster is something nasty that happens to somebody else. Look it up on the Internet: there are as many different definitions of the words *catastrophe, disaster,* and *emergency* as there are Web sites that define them.

For those who need some coaching on the nature of disasters, here are some searing truths: Recent events (9/11, Katrina, bird flu) have reminded us, even in our protected cocoons of technological sophistication and prosperity, that we are virtually powerless in the face of nature and that an entire region of the country (e.g., New Orleans) can go from normality to catastrophe in the blink of an eye. Major disasters are a recurring fact of life for every generation, and the fact that we have not been visited by major disasters in the United States for two centuries only means that we are long overdue. The fact is that we are not much more prepared in a practical sense to survive a long-term widespread disaster than our poorer counterparts in other countries who deal with similar situations on a daily basis. The only way we seem to relate to disasters is vicariously through the unrealistic eyes of Hollywood, with their asteroids and living-dead epidemics, and their superheroes who save us from certain doom.

Let's take a look at some real disasters. There's a long list to choose from, so let's stick with disasters that have occurred since 1900. Here's a brief glimpse of a few modern catastrophes:

First on the list is war, and for our purposes we'll list World War I and II together. Starting in 1914 and until the Japanese surrender in 1945, this disaster resulted in the deaths of 70 million people, most of them civilians. It included some amazingly cruel stuff, like the Rape of Nanking, the Holocaust, the atomic bombing of Hiroshima and Nagasaki, the bombing of Dresden, the sinking of the *Lusitania* and the *Wilhelm Gustloff*. The effects of this disaster will linger for centuries, as have the effects of other wars. Look at the Crusades. Christian crusaders took Jerusalem and slaughtered everyone in the city—90,000 people. Nine hundred years later we see the indirect results: terrorists bringing down our skyscrapers and our young people being blown up with improvised explosive devices in the streets of Baghdad.

In 1918 an influenza pandemic broke out. It may or may not have started in Europe, but it really took hold when it was spread by the troops fighting or preparing to fight in World War I. By 1919 it had killed 70 million people, second only to the worst episode of the plague in the Middle Ages, which killed 75 million in thirteen years. In the United States the influenza killed over half a million. Most Americans would tell you that such an event can't happen again because of our superior medical understanding. The truth is that we still don't have a cure for influenza. It still kills thousands of Americans every year, and some nasty new strains are worrisome to health officials. We know little more about the virus than we did after the 1918 pandemic. Another virus, HIV (AIDS), will kill 90 million in Africa alone by 2025, and malaria continues to kill a million people each year. Pandemics are continuous, and it is unlikely that we will ever be pandemic-free.

The Hwang He and Yangtze rivers floods in 1931 killed 140,000 Chinese. But the real killers were the resulting famine and disease, which killed another 3 million.

The Chinese famine of the late 1950s killed 40 million people. It could be considered the worst man-made disaster of the century because it was caused in large part by agricultural reforms mandated by the Chinese government.

Floods continue to kill with remarkable effectiveness. The 1970 Bangladesh cyclone saw 500,000 die in the storm surge.

The Indian Ocean tsunami just after Christmas of 2004 killed a quarter of a million people, many of them Westerners on vacation. It was the worst tsunami ever recorded and was caused by a large undersea earthquake.

Hardly a day goes by without news of an earthquake somewhere. The Kashmir and Pakistan earthquake of 2005 killed 100,000.

When you glance at the brief descriptions of these and other disasters it should become obvious that there can be an enormous list of bad after-effects from large disasters. The big killers are famine, disease, and flooding. Flooding almost always leads to ruined crops, famine, and disease. Earthquakes lead to tsunamis and turn cities into infernos. Volcanoes cause tsunamis and can spew enough debris into the atmosphere to cause major drops in the world temperature, leading to famine and disease. Nuclear and chemical disasters can kill for years.

Another uncomfortable truth stares us in the face as we look at the recent history of disaster: technological disasters are increasing as our reliance on technology increases. Bhopal, Chernobyl, the atomic bombings of Hiroshima and Nagasaki, and large-scale computer crime foreshadow the disasters we will face in the future. Global warming is an ominous natural event fueled by man's disregard that has the potential to generate major catastrophes.

We have some very recent reminders of our vulnerability: terrorism, the threats of SARS and avian influenza, the turmoil the entire nation experienced with a hurricane in a small region of the country that killed fewer than 2,000 people. These things remind us that we need to be ready. Nothing has changed. Disasters always have happened and always will happen. A key to peace of mind is preparation. Another key is taking responsibility. Every disaster starts at the individual level. It then becomes a local responsibility, then a state problem, and then, if the disaster is big enough, a federal responsibility. During and after Katrina, public outrage was aimed at the wrong people. Your safety is ultimately your own responsibility. The fate of a city is the mayor's responsibility. A state is the governor's responsibility. Blame for Katrina immediately went right to the top. The scapegoating conveniently let individuals, city officials, and state agencies off the hook for their own failures to prepare for the disaster and to enforce measures to protect the people they were responsible for.

You can live your life in denial and blame others for your own failures. The lazy among us will most certainly do that. The smart ones will prepare and take responsibility for themselves.

Different experts classify disasters in their own ways. For simplicity we'll divide them into *Natural Disasters* and *Man-made Disasters.*

Natural Disasters

Natural disasters are the most consistently catastrophic in terms of shear death toll. These include earthquakes, volcanoes, floods, cyclones and hurricanes, tornadoes, droughts, and slope failures. We are essentially powerless against these disasters except for mitigation and effective response, and they often produce horrific effects well outside of the immediate area they first occur in. Impoverished areas suffer grossly higher death tolls due to their architectural inferiorities and deficits in their medical systems, then disease and famine follow.

Although flooding generates high death tolls, famine and disease take the prize for the biggest killers. Often the three work in combination. Aside from the initial drownings, flooding causes sewage and drinking water to mix. Rotting corpses add to the water pollution and disease inventory. The most prevalent diseases are gastrointestinal diseases that characteristically cause severe dehydration (e.g., cholera), which, in turn, cannot be relieved adequately because of the lack of clean water.

The interesting thing about disasters involving disease is the ominous way in which they show up. Diseases usually emerge over a wide area and over a long period of time. They're often not treated as disasters until the media picks up on the situation, and then public opinion forces government officials to take action. By the time the full gravity of the situation is realized, the disease is out of control.

Man-Made Disasters

These are the disasters that are caused by humans through negligence, technological failure, fanaticism, or shear mean-heartedness. Fire, war, and religious fanaticism have been the traditional causes of these kinds of disasters, but other common causes include civil unrest, building collapse, industrial accidents, and transportation accidents. As we urbanize and our capacity to produce, store, and transport hazardous materials and technologies grows, so does the potential intensity of a disaster.

3.   The Truth About Disaster Planning

Disaster planning is discussed in some detail later in this book. For now I'll leave you with the following fact-based opinion.

A list of potential disasters would be larger than this book. But the effects of all disasters have some things in common, and it's these common effects that we need to prepare for. It's like making cakes. Cake is flour, sugar, salt, eggs, milk, shortening, and a little baking soda or baking powder. There's a basic procedure for mixing and baking cake. Some pots and pans, bowls and spoons, and an oven are needed to make cake. We have this all put together in one kitchen. It wouldn't make sense to have separate kitchens, each with its own ingredients and its own pots and pans and utensils, for each kind of cake we might bake—one kitchen for lemon cake, another for chocolate cake. That's often the problem with both individual and government disaster planning, especially within government health agencies. Commonly each disaster is planned for individually, and a different "kitchen" and procedure is developed for every type of disaster. Plans get way too complicated, and soon the collection of individual plans is too bulky and complicated to be practical. Unfortunately, this is where a lot of public money has been wasted since the federal government started dumping money into the local and regional emergency management systems and the health departments as a result of 9/11 and the war on terrorism.

Although in the United States some definite progress has been made in preparation for terrorism and disaster response, an enormous amount of money has been wasted on redundant, repeated projects and inefficient handling of training and materials. Turf wars between agencies and individual egos get in the way of progress, and endless conventions and conferences in lavish hotels drain the coffers that you fill with your tax money. Many of the individuals hired to carry out projects are either unqualified for the jobs they are assigned to or are siphoned off into other work not directly related to disaster planning. There is little oversight and little incentive to improve this situation. In the end, your best bet is to prepare yourself and be pleasantly surprised if the government response is good, rather than to make no personal preparations and expect an immediate response from overwhelmed and inefficient government agencies.

Chapter 1
Emergency Management

It certainly makes sense for us all to be aware of the inner workings of the emergency planners and responders whose job it is to save us in a disaster.

1.   Phases of Emergency Management

Emergency planners and managers are concerned with the four phases of a disaster: mitigation, preparedness, response, and recovery. These phases also relate to individuals, families, and businesses in the plans they make.

Mitigation consists of action that prevents disasters from occurring, or actions that limit the damage done by disasters when they happen. Mitigation is based on risk assessments. Mitigation may be related to structure or location, and very often includes insurance protection.

The preparedness phase is when action or response plans are developed, and resources are identified and stockpiled.

In the response phase, professional and volunteer emergency services teams and organizations mobilize and respond to the actual disaster. Individuals and families might shelter in place or evacuate during this phase.

The recovery phase starts when the immediate threats to life have passed. The disaster may still be in progress, and the recovery may take weeks, months, or years. The recovery phases takes into consideration both the restoration of daily life to normal, as well as mitigation of future disasters. In other words, now that you know what needs to be done to survive the next disaster, get it done.

2.   Emergency & Disaster Professionals and Volunteers

Professional emergency managers come from diversified backgrounds and are responsible for government and community mitigation, preparedness, response and recovery. Typically in the United States emergency management positions were political in nature and a manager with real experience in emergency response and disaster management was the exception rather than the rule. The typical manager has had a background in law enforcement or fire service, but little or no experience in emergency planning. Since 9/11 the trend has been either to hire managers with specific emergency management training or require managers to acquire specific training in office. The result has been a relative increase in the competence of emergency management. There are now professional associations for emergency managers, and some professional certifications are now available.

At the front line of any disaster are the actual first responders: the fire service, law enforcement, and emergency medical services.

Essentially, law enforcement is responsible for civil tranquility and security as well as crime prevention, investigation, and surveillance. In many rural areas, local law enforcement is responsible for search and rescue. Many law enforcement agencies include specialized teams, such as bomb and SWAT squads. Law enforcement also includes state and federal police.

The fire service is typically responsible for fire suppression, hazardous materials operations, and search and rescue. Firefighters are usually trained to standard levels as Firefighter 1 through 3, and for hazardous materials operations through technician levels. Their HAZMAT training and equipment give them varying capabilities to identify and contain chemical, biological, radiological, and explosive hazards.

Emergency medical services (EMS) are the ground, boat, or aircraft ambulances and the EMTs, paramedics, nurses, and doctors that staff them. In many cities these services are provided by the fire department. A basic EMT is required to undergo about 120 hours of training before testing for certification. Basic EMTs provide what's called basic life support (BLS) or, more simply, advanced first aid with basic airway adjuncts and automated defibrillation. Intermediate EMTs add on an additional 40 to 200 hours of training, depending on the state requirements, and can typically administer a half-dozen medications, start simple IVs, and insert advanced airways. Paramedics undergo about 1,200 hours of additional training and provide Advanced Life Support (ALS), which includes EKG interpretation, electrical cardiac therapies, advanced airways, advanced IV lines, two to three dozen drugs, and a number of lifesaving invasive or surgical procedures.

All emergency responder agencies that have been granted federal funds are now required to use the Incident Command System (ICS) as their management system for emergency operations. The ICS provides a common framework within which different responding agencies can work together, using common terminology. It's designed to shrink or expand according to the situation, and it immediately answers the question of who's in charge (the Incident Commander or IC).

The ICS is a part of the National Incident Management System (NIMS), which is under the National Response

Plan (NRP). The National Response Plan is the nation's plan for response to national disasters. In the United States disaster response and planning is first a local government responsibility. When local government exhausts its resources, it then asks for additional resources from the county level. The request process goes similarly from the county to the state to the federal level as additional resource needs are identified. Under the NRP, federal resources will integrate with local, county, state, or tribal authorities in a unified command structure. Management will continue to be handled at the lowest possible level.

In addition to professional and volunteer law enforcement or fire and EMS personnel, local primary responders may include the health department for early health/medical response and assistance in investigation. It may also eventually include professional and volunteer relief agencies (such as the Red Cross) to provide first aid, supportive care, and basic needs assistance, and federally supported community-based volunteer teams such as the Community Emergency Response Teams (CERT) and the regional Medical Reserve Corps (MRC). Community Emergency Response Teams are a Citizen Corps program focused on disaster preparedness and teaching basic disaster response skills. These volunteer teams are utilized to provide emergency support when disaster overwhelms the conventional emergency services. They are trained to perform basic fire supression, light search-and-rescue, basic first aid, and triage. The Medical Reserve Corps (MRC) Program coordinates the skills of practicing and retired physicians, nurses, EMS and other health professionals as well as other citizens interested in health issues, who volunteer to help their community during large-scale emergency situations.

This, of course, is not a complete list of responders that you'll find in your community. In the United States we are incredibly lucky to have such a large and skilled cadre of professional and volunteer organizations.

3.   Personal & Family Emergency Management

Most disasters happen suddenly and without any warning, and the effects can linger for years. The immediate effects may include the loss of water, gas, electricity, and telephone service. Emergency services will be so overwhelmed that they may not be available to you for hours or days. To ensure your safety and well-being and that of your family, most government organizations and NGOs (non-government organizations) recommend that you stockpile 72 hours worth of supplies to handle your basic needs. They also recommend that you make a simple plan, train with your family on an occasional basis, and make minor structural modifications within the home. A smaller version of the preparedness kit is recommended for the family car. We'll go over all of this in detail in the following chapters.

Practically speaking, in a long-term widespread disaster a 72-hour kit would not be enough. As water, food, shelter, and comfort items become harder to find, they may become precious commodities with a higher trade value than cash. In a worst-case scenario, we would be bartering with these items, and those who have them will be in a far better position to survive than those who don't. Seen in that light, a two-year supply makes incredibly good sense.

Let's go back to the idea of stockpiling materials to meet your basic needs. What are your basic needs?

Although we all have our specialty and comfort items that we think we can't live without, the basic needs all fit under Maslow's hierarchy—a subject that we all slept through in Psych 101. The basic concept is that the higher needs only come into focus once all the needs that are lower down in the pyramid are satisfied. The lower levels of needs are the most primitive, and without sastisfying them we cannot obtain the upper-level needs.

In planning for a disaster our primary goal should be to prepare the means for ourselves and our loved ones to satisfy the needs within the lower two levels for the duration of the disaster. This equates to simple *survival*. Survive first. Everything else is icing on the cake. The touchy feely group hugs and fireside Kumbaya hymns can come later.

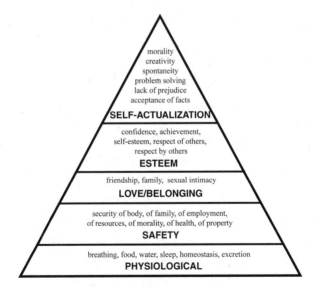

Maslow's hierarchy of needs

4.   Business Emergency Management

Small businesses are the foundation of America's economy. According to Ready.gov, small businesses account for more than 99 percent of all companies with employees, employ 50 percent of all private sector workers, and provide nearly 45 percent of the nation's payroll. Businesses, large and small, must be ready to survive and recover to ensure personal, local, and national economies and to protect our business investments.

Doing nothing is not an option. Experience shows that even relatively short-term disruption can destroy a business. It also shows that disasters in one part of the world can shut down businesses in another. Some relatively simple pre-planning can avoid this.

5.   International & National Organizations

Red Cross/Red Crescent

National Red Cross/Red Crescent societies often have important roles in responding to disasters. Additionally, the International Federation of Red Cross and Red Crescent Societies (IFRC) may send assessment teams to an affected country.

United Nations

United Nations responsibility for disaster response rests with the resident coordinator in the effected country. The international response will be coordinated, if requested by the country's government, by the UN Office for the

Coordination of Humanitarian Affairs (UN-OCHA). It may send a UN Disaster Assessment and Coordination (UNDAC) team.

United States

Under the Department of Homeland Security (DHS), the Federal Emergency Management Agency (FEMA) is the lead agency for emergency management. The United States and its territories are all within one of ten FEMA regions. Tribal, state, county, and local governments develop emergency management programs/departments and operate hierarchically within each region. Emergencies are managed at the most local level possible, utilizing mutual aid agreements with adjacent jurisdictions.

If the emergency is terrorist related or if declared an "Incident of National Significance," the Secretary of Homeland Security will initiate the National Response Plan (NRP). Under this plan the involvement of federal resources will be made possible, integrating with the local, county, state, or tribal entities. Management will continue to be handled at the lowest possible level utilizing the National Incident Management System (NIMS).

The Federal Bureau of Investigation is responsible for criminal investigation and assitance with lab testing in terrorist incidents.

The Department of Health and Human Services tracks and reports health data, does medical investigation, manages medical and pharmaceutical stockpiles, exercises powers to quarantine or isolate, and provides public health advice. Agencies within GHHS may also investigate or assist in the investigation of an event.

The Environmental Protection Agency tracks environmental contamination and helps manage major chemical incidents.

The Department of Energy provides radiological testing and response.

The Citizen Corps is an organization of volunteer service programs, administered locally and coordinated nationally by DHS, which seek to mitigate disaster and prepare the population for emergency response through public education, training, and outreach. Community Emergency Response Teams (CERT), Fire Corps teams, and Medical Reserve Corps (MRC) teams are Citizen Corps programs focused on disaster preparedness and teaching basic disaster response skills. These volunteer teams are utilized to provide emergency support when disaster overwhelms the conventional emergency services.

Canada

Public Safety and Emergency Preparedness Canada (PSEPC) is Canada's equivalent of FEMA. Each province has an emergency management office and most local levels of government have similar offices. PSEPC also coordinates and supports the efforts of federal organizations ensuring national security and safety. It also works with other levels of government, first responders, community groups, the private sector (operators of critical infrastructure) and other nations.

PSEPC's work is based on a wide range of policies and legislation. The Public Safety and Emergency Preparedness Act defines the powers, duties, and functions of PSEPC. Other acts are specific to fields such as corrections,

MRC ops center during a flood response in the four-corners
area of the Southwest.

emergency management, law enforcement, and national
security.

6.   What the Government Does and Doesn't Want You to Know

The government is very open about what it *does* want
you to know about disaster preparedness. The FEMA and
CDC Web sites and Ready.gov are full of educational and
media materials. FEMA's Emergency Management Institute
(EMI) is an incredible source of independent-study training
that is accessible to anyone. It's probably one of FEMA's
crowning achievements, and professionals and laypersons
alike should take advantage of what's offered there.

Obviously, what the government *does not* want you to know is not so easily accessible. Censorship is not dead and the government can and will withhold whatever it wants from the public under the rationalization that it's in the interest of national security. Sometimes these withholdings are under the guise of preventing public panic. Other times they're for the protection of sensitive resources. But more often than not, the information you don't get is withheld because of the political ramifications of wasted funds, costly procrastinations, and potential lawsuits. Politicians don't want egg on their faces, or the wrath of angry citizens. This public information deficit is especially bad in the realms of emerging infections, terrorism, and government corruption.

This being the case, where do we turn for our information? Unfortunately the answer is the Internet and media. This is sad, because the first resource is subject to fanaticism and exaggeration, and the second is subject to outright bias. All things considered, the best resource is our own common sense, and the best action items are simple plans that focus on the hierarchy of needs and that include lifestyles encompassing universal keys to longevity (e.g., proper hygiene, continuing education, etc).

Chapter 2
Basic Personal Preparedness

A quick search on the Internet will bring up dozens of sites with excellent information on how to prepare yourself and your family for disasters. Each lists a number of steps to take to ensure adequate preparation. Although the steps may be in different order, they all have these components in common:

1. Getting information about local hazards and the emergencies that you and your family are most likely to encounter
2. Detailing family communication strategies
3. Learning how to shut off utilities
4. Developing, rehearsing, and maintaining an emergency plan
5. Assembling disaster supplies kits
6. Gaining familiarity with community warning systems and evacuation routes
7. Learning where to seek shelter and how to shelter-in-place
8. Learning about community, school, and workplace disaster plans

If you don't read any other chapter in this book, read this one. We'll go through the basic steps here and provide some simple ideas that will help you develop a reasonable plan and make other practical preparations.

1.   Knowing About Local Hazards

Contact the local emergency management office (usually a county office), the Red Cross, and local responder offices (police, fire, emergency medical services, health department) for information on local hazards. Don't expect a personally guided tour and lots of individual attention. These offices are busy and probably have already prepared some printed information. If you need more detail, get it from the Internet by going to state disaster management sites (state homeland security), or from other sites, like the FEMA and CDC websites, that have specific hazards information. Both of these sites have detailed information on the recent history of disaster declarations and health emergencies in each state. The FEMA and EPA sites have hazard map databases. The FEMA map site moves like cold molasses and can be confusing, so be patient.

The purpose of this research is to establish what the prominent hazards are and what disaster-related emergencies are most likely to occur. As you learn about them, log them in the following template and add notes to customize the information:

Hazard or Emergency	Likelihood or Risk of occurring (None, low, moderate, high)	Steps to reduce risk
Drought	High (in progress)	Reduce watering schedule
Flood	Moderate	
Fire	Low but constant	Smoke detectors in home
Hazardous materials • Chemical spills • Hazardous waste (White Mesa Mill)		

2.   The Family Communications Plan

Families may not be together when a disaster occurs, and events can easily pull families apart. All members of the family should know how to make contact with other family members and designated contacts outside the neighborhood and out of state. These are persons who your family can notify that they are safe and where they are located.

A critical part of communication is face-to-face contact. The family should designate a meeting place outside the home for home emergencies and local disasters, and another outside the neighborhood for more widespread problems. Establish phone and cell numbers as well as e-mail addresses for these contacts and numbers for emergency services (poison control, 911, etc.).

It's easy to put all these numbers and locations on a contact card that can be given to each family member and each designated contact to carry with them. Keep one by each house phone, and send one to school and one to your boss. Also include a copy in each disaster kit.

3.   Shutting Off Utilities

If your home or building is structurally damaged, you may need to turn the utilities off to prevent fires and other additional damage. It's also possible that your local authorities will ask you to turn off utilities. Before any such event, you should teach family members how to locate and safely shut off the utilities.

Shutting Off Electricity

Electricity can electrocute you or to create sparks that can ignite a natural gas leak or spilled flammables. To shut off electricity:

- Find the circuit boxes. There may be more than one. They may be equipped with fuses or circuit breakers. With fuses you should find a knife switch handle or pullout fuse marked "MAIN." If your house has circuit breakers open the metal door of the breaker box. The main circuit breaker should be clearly marked showing on and off positions.

- Remove all the small fuses or turn off all the small breakers before shutting off the main circuit breaker.

- If you have sub-panels adjacent to the main fuse or breaker panel or in other parts of the house shut them off before you shut of the main.

Shutting Off the Gas

If you don't smell gas or you don't have severe damage to your home you should not have to shut the gas off. It's your decision, but remember that natural gas fires and explosions commonly occur in damaged structures and pipelines. Shutoff procedures may be different from region to region and according to the metering device. Talk to the local gas company for advice.

If you smell or hear leaking gas, get out immediately. Open a window on the way out if possible to do so without wasting time. Turn off the gas main outside. Tell the gas company about the leak.

The main gas shutoff is usually located outside with the gas meter, on a pipe coming out of the ground into the gas meter. If the gas meter is located in a cabinet enclosure built into the building or located inside the building, the gas service shutoff valve will be outside on a section of gas service pipe next to the building near the gas meter, or in an

Not all circuit boxes look the same. This box has individual
breakers above and below the "main" breaker.

underground box in the sidewalk. If you live in an apartment
or dormitory or rent an office in a large building, there may
be multiple meters with individual shutoff valves near the
gas meters, and a master valve for the entire building where
the gas pipe comes out of the ground. Ask your landlord
which is yours.

Turn the valve crosswise to the pipe using a 12- to
15-inch adjustable pipe or crescent-type wrench or other
suitable tool.

All the pilot lights in your building will go out when you
turn the valve off. You will need to have the gas company or

A main gas shutoff valve. When the holes are aligned, the
valve can be padlocked closed.

another qualified individual (plumber, contractor, or trained
homeowner) relight every pilot when turning the gas back
on. Not relighting all the pilot lights could result in a gas
buildup and explosion in your home.

Clear the area around the main gas shutoff valve and
mark the valve in fluorescent duct tape or paint for quick
and easy access in case of emergency. A wrench should be
attached to a pipe next to the shutoff valve or in another
accessible location nearby.

Shutting Off Water Lines

Broken water lines can cause severe damage and can spread
disease. Precious water can be lost at a rate of 15 gallons per
minute from a single house line.
Steps for shutting off water:

- Find the shutoff valve where it enters the house or where it ties into the municipal water system. If it's from a municipal supply it probably will have a water meter and shutoff valve grouped together near the street in an underground access hatch. Inside the hatch you will find either a handle or a valve with a straight metal flange across the top. The handle maybe a wheel or a paddle. Turn it until it won't turn anymore. Remember: "righty tighty, lefty loosy." If the valve has a metal flange, use a pipe wrench to operate. It should close with a quarter turn. If a wrench is required, leave one near the valve for emergencies.
- A rusty valve will be difficult or impossible to close, so check it *before* an emergency.
- Plainly label the valve.

Most homes have other shut off valves that can shut off sections of the water supply. You may find a hose bib and a shutoff valve where the water main enters your house. In cold weather locations the shutoff may be in the basement or inside the house. This valve will typically shut off all water inside the house but not outside.

4. Developing an Emergency Plan

Your plan is going to include the hazards list we just described and all of the information included in the eight common planning steps. It should contain information on warning systems and signals, including the Emergency Alert System and NOAA Weather Radio, safety plans, communications plans, escape and evacuation routes and guidelines, integration of community and school plans, awareness of workplace plans, insurance and vital record data, plans for special needs and pets, and the assembly and storage of disaster supply kits.

The key ingredients to your personal and family plan are:

1. Identifying a meeting place for your family near your home and another outside your neighborhood.

2. Picking an out-of-state contact (friend or relative) and another who lives nearby as your family contacts.

3. Developing a contact list for every family member, including work, school, and cell phone numbers.

4. Giving your family information to family contacts.

5. Posting clear written directions to your home in a convenient location in the event you need to call emergency services. The directions can be read over the phone when calling for help.

6. Developing and sharing with your family a clear fire escape policy and plan.

7. Showing each family member how to turn off utilities, and showing them the location of emergency equipment, including fire extinguishers, first aid kits, and disaster supplies.

8. Finding out how your kids' schools will handle crisis situations.

9. Giving the school your contact information, including your other designated contacts.

10. Learning where students will be taken if they are evacuated, how the school will notify you, and how you will meet your child.

5. Disaster Supply Kits

Surviving after a disaster may mean having to provide your own food and water for several days. Basic utilities could be cut off for weeks. You may need to evacuate and leave the comforts of home behind. When the disaster is forecast, the store shelves will be empty by the time the disaster strikes. If not forecasted, the shelves will be inaccessible after the disaster occurs.

It's smart to have different kits for home, work, and in the car. The government would like you to build a home kit that has enough food, water, and essential supplies to see you and your family through at least three days. I recommend more. It's not unreasonable to put away enough supplies to see you through three weeks or even three months. In a worst-case scenario, your supply can be bartered as well as eaten.

Your kit at work should contain at least a one-day supply of essentials. It should include a change of clothing, stout shoes, and should be packed with the idea in mind that conditions will be colder, wetter, and darker than it is on the day you first packed it. Keep it in a backpack, ready to grab when needed.

A *basic three-day house kit* might consist of the following items:

- ☐ Containers to pack it all in. Several small containers would be easier to move than one or two big ones. Large buckets or small garbage cans can be used for carrying water, portable potties, wash basins.
- ☐ Three-day supply of non-perishable food—three meals per person and pet per day (see chapter 8).

☐ Three-day supply of water—one gallon of drinkable water per person and pet per day (see chapter 7).

☐ Portable battery- or crank-powered radio or television and extra batteries. Replace batteries annually.

☐ LED flashlight or headlamp with extra batteries for each person.

☐ First aid kit and notes (see chapter 9).

☐ Sanitation and hygiene items (moist towelettes, toilet paper, washcloth, towel, soap, hand sanitizer, razors, contact lens solution, feminine supplies, sunscreen, insect repellent, small mirror).

☐ Matches and waterproof container.

☐ Whistle.

☐ Multi-tool pocket knife.

☐ Extra clothing. One complete change per person, including socks, undies, shirt, and pants.

☐ Cold climate items: change of clothing for each person, including:
  ○ Shell parka
  ○ Insulating coat (fleece) or sweater
  ○ Hat
  ○ Mitten or gloves
  ○ Sleeping bag or warm blanket(s)

☐ Kitchen accessories and cooking utensils, including a can opener.

☐ Photocopies of credit cards, identification cards, driver's license, passport, immunizations records, wills, deeds, stocks, bonds, contracts, bank numbers, and inventories.

☐ Cash. Try for a minimum of $25 per person per day. Traveler's checks are an inferior second choice. Credit cards.

☐ Specialty items:
  ○ Prescription medications
  ○ Eye glasses, contact lens solution
  ○ Hearing aid batteries
  ○ Denture supplies
  ○ Small sewing kit
☐ Infant items: formula, diapers, bottles, pacifiers.
☐ Small entertainment items (paperback books, etc.).
☐ Extra house and car keys.
☐ Paper goods and pens, pencils.
☐ Local telephone directory.
☐ Family contacts card.
☐ Contractor-weight trash bags (for garbage sacks, emergency shelters, emergency rain coats, potty liners).
☐ Fire extinguisher.
☐ Work gloves.
☐ Camp shovel.
☐ Cooking stove and fuel.
☐ Cooking utensils.
☐ Mess kit.
☐ Dishwashing soap.

A *car kit* is wise to have not just for disasters, but for simple mini-tragedies like getting stranded. It should contain the essentials for a day or two, also planning for wetter and colder weather, as well as some road gear like flares and jumper cables. Note that battery-operated safety flares with multiple flashing LEDs are now available. You might also include a small tool kit, an inverter, a GPS (if you know how to use one) and extra batteries, a roll of bright surveyors' tape, a tire repair kit and a can of tire sealant, an electric tire inflator, a tow line, and a five-pound bag of salt or sand.

A Warning About Gadgets

Don't confuse preparedness with paranoia. Somebody out there is making money off paranoia, selling us all kinds of gadgets we won't need. At best they're worthless. At worst they're dangerous. Before you spend money on exotic items, ask yourself these questions:

- Do I really need it?
- Can I get a better price somewhere else?
- Does this salesman know what he's talking about?

Let's look, for instance, at gas masks. Masks are pricey, and you have to know how to put them on and maintain them if they're going to do you any good. And are you really going to carry that thing around with you every day? Even if you just happen to have it with you when something happens, chances are you won't know until it's too late. Or you'll have the wrongs filters. Or you won't remember how to put it on and fit it properly to get a seal.

Another great example is the skyscraper parachute escape kit. We'll chat about that one a bit later in the book.

6.   Community Warning Systems and Evacuation Routes

The Emergency Alert System is a nationwide method of alerting the public to disasters. Federal regulations require all TV and radio broadcast stations and cable stations to participate in EAS tests and activations. EAS was designed to be a cooperative effort between government agencies and local broadcasters. EAS is the fastest and most reliable way to alert large areas or isolated locations to major emergencies.

The EAS consists of a network of broadcast stations across the nation with equipment designed to allow the automatic transmission and broadcasting of emergency messages. Alerts pass from station to station and on to the air automatically, without human intervention. The state offices of Homeland Security and Emergency Management activate the EAS for state-level alerts.

The EAS incorporates coding that allows specific locations to be alerted, so that only affected areas receive the alert, so as not to alarm locations not affected. The EAS allows alert information to be digitally coded, along with standard audio information, so that television stations can have a screen crawl that displays the text of the alert.

The National Oceanic and Atmospheric Administration (NOAA) Weather Radio (NWR) is a nationwide network of radio stations that broadcast continuous weather information to specifically configured radio receivers. Many ham, GMRS, and FRS radios are also configured to receive NWR. NWR weather forecasts are regional, and not all regions are covered. To find out if your region is covered, go to nws.noa.gov.

The National Weather Service (NWS) broadcasts warnings, watches, forecasts, and other non-weather related hazard information 24 hours a day. During an emergency, NWS forecasters interrupt routine broadcasts and send a special tone activating local weather radios. Weather radios equipped with a special alarm tone feature sound an alert to give you immediate information about a life-threatening situation.

NWR broadcasts warnings and post-event information for all types of hazards: weather (e.g., tornadoes, floods), natural (e.g., earthquakes, forest fires, and volcanic activity), technological (e.g., chemical releases, oil spills, nuclear power plant emergencies), and national emergencies (e.g., terrorist attacks). Working with other federal agencies and the Federal Communications Commission's (FCC) Emergency Alert System (EAS), NWR is an all-hazards radio network, making it the most comprehensive weather and emergency information available to the public.

Use the following template to provide warning system information for you and your community:

Warning System	Actions
Emergency Alert System (EAS) stations:	
NOAA Weather Radio (NWR):	
Community warning systems: Sirens Telephone (reverse 911)	
Web sites	

When necessary, local officials will provide specific information through the media, sirens, telephone, or loudspeaker. Check with local agencies to determine emergency evacuation routes. There may also be times when you decide on your own that you need to leave your current location. Here are some standard evacuation guidelines:

Planning	Essential response	Additional actions
Maintain your vehicle with at least a half tank of gas. Make transportation arrangements with a friend or local government if you don't own a car.	Keep a full tank of gas if evacuation seems likely.	Bring along your disaster kit(s), including medical histories and important documents.
Plan multiple routes out of your area. Write them down in your plan. Remember, local emergency management may issue specific instructions and evacuation routes Know the local TV and radio stations, and tune in for information and instructions.	Listen to a battery- or crank-powered radio and follow local evacuation instructions.	Wear sturdy clothes and shoes that provide protection. Close and lock doors and windows. Unplug electrical equipment. Leave refrigerators and freezers plugged in unless there's a flood risk.
	Gather your family and go immediately if you are instructed to do so. Leave early enough to avoid being trapped by severe weather and traffic. Follow recommended evacuation routes. Do not take shortcuts; they may be blocked. Watch for washed-out roads and bridges. Do not drive into flooded areas. Stay away from downed power lines.	Let someone know where you are going.

7. Learn about Shelters and Shelter in Place

Shelter may consist of hunkering down in your own home or office, staying with friends or relatives, hotel lodging, or staying in a mass care facility operated by the government or a relief organization.

If you decide to shelter at home, you need to consider a number of things: meeting water needs, food, and safety.

Mass care shelters will normally provide food and basic bathroom facilities, and possibly basic medical care. Even so, you will want to bring your disaster supplies kit(s) along with you. It not only provides security if food becomes scarce, but it's also a means of barter when money means virtually nothing.

Group dynamics in a mass shelter can be tough. It can be crowded. It's important to have a command structure, and everyone is expected to cooperate with the shelter manager and anyone else who is providing assistance. Alcoholic beverages, weapons, and recreational drugs should be strictly forbidden in any shelter. A safety guard and a communications person should be on duty and awake at all times.

Plan on staying in the shelter until local authorities give the all clear.

8. Integrate Community, School, and Workplace Plans

Ask the local emergency manager if there's a disaster plan for the community or county. They will always tell you yes, whether they have one or not. Rural communities are notorious for keeping their plans "in the head" of the local sheriff or mayor. If they do say yes, ask them how to obtain a copy. For security purposes many communities are restricting their plans on a "need to know" basis. Do not be offended if you don't get a look at the plan. If you do get to see it, take note of what it contains and what hazards it covers. Look for what pertains to you and your family. Also note how often it's supposed to be updated. If it looks out of date, mention it to someone.

Again, ask the administrators of your child's school or day care about their emergency plan. Get specific information about how the school will communicate with families during an emergency, and how they plan to feed and care for the kids when the school is locked down or the kids are sheltering in place. Also, inquire about evacuation and sheltering procedures.

Note that in light of recent events schools are under particular pressure to lock down the facility and maintain a strict accounting of each child in the event of a crisis. It's likely that you will not be able to get in to sign out or talk to your child until the lockdown is terminated. Emergency officials and the media will issue instructions.

If you have not already been given adequate information about your workplace emergency plan, ask your boss to show you the plan or to explain to you specifically what the plan is and how you fit into it.

9.   Records and Property Inventory

Part of your planning should be to collect and inventory vital records. These include:

- Insurance policies.

- Deeds and property records.
- Contracts.
- Important financial records not saved electronically.
- Medical records for each member of the family. This medical record should include: name, allergies, medications, immunizations, and medical history (any problem that has been or could be a threat to life or limb).
- Birth certificates.

These records should be kept at least in a waterproof container, and at best in a safety box.

10. Insurance

Insurance is a gamble that buys peace of mind. It's a transfer of risk, from us to the insurance company that is supposed to protect us against financially damaging events. We are gambling that the insurance company will cover us when something bad happens. They are gambling that nothing bad will happen, or if it does, that we won't make a claim. It's risky. Often the decision about whether to be insured isn't ours to make. It may be too expensive or the insurance company may simply refuse to cover us. And even if we do get insured, most of us don't understand exactly how we're covered or what we're covered for. Most unsuccessful claims are submitted in good faith by policy holders who really thought they were covered, and they are denied based on some obscure exclusion or exception in the policy that takes the customer by surprise. And if you do make a successful claim, you may lose your policy or your rates may soar. Insurance companies determine their rates largely on location, structure, risk, and property value. Other factors used to determine your eligibility or rates are credit scores, occupation, marital status, and discriminatory factors such as gender and level of education and whether you've filed a claim before. It can seem horribly unfair and downright unethical, but that's the nature of gambling.

For anyone thinking about disaster insurance, there are five major factors that will determine the availability of the insurance and your willingness to pay for it. They are *finances, location, the type and age of the structure, its dollar value,* and *your level of comfort.* Your choice to purchase insurance should be based on those factors and backed up by a sound awareness of what your policy does and doesn't promise to do.

The first thing you should do is examine your current homeowner's insurance policy to determine exactly what it will cover. Discuss any questions with your insurance agent. Once you've done that, then find out where and how you can get more coverage. This, of course, will depend on the type of disaster you're trying to insure against. Most policies don't cover flooding and earthquakes. Your insurance company may not insure you against other disasters that your location is particularly at risk for. In that case, you'll have to go hunting for coverage.

Keep in mind that many insurance policies only cover structural damage to the home, and not damage to landscaping, outbuildings, or septic and sewer systems.

After looking around you may decide to purchase new insurance or modify your old policy. If you decide to NOT have insurance make sure your reasons are sound. Often the reasons are one or more of the following: high prices (premiums), high deductibles that must be paid before the insurance applies, inadequate coverage, no legal or mortgage requirement to insure, or reliance on the government and relief agencies to help.

If you believe the government and relief agencies are going to pull your ass out of the financial fire, think again. The majority of disasters are not declared states of emergency by the president, which has to be done before the Federal Emergency Management Agency and the Small Business Administration step in and offer assistance. The federal grants will not have to be paid back, but they are very limited and generally reserved for those who are not insured. Loans must be paid back, and will add to your overall financial burden on the property. Also, loans are restricted to the amount that your insurance doesn't cover. And you can expect that the shortages of construction materials and contractors that occur after a disaster will result in inflated repair costs. In the end, you are not likely to break even on your losses.

If you're thinking that you might not purchase insurance, here are some other considerations before making that decision:

- Are you downplaying the risk in your area? Many, if not most, homeowners and builders are in denial about the risks the scientists and local emergency managers have warned them about. Ninety percent of the country's population lives in active earthquake fault zones and most don't even know it. Many live in hurricane zones and simply choose to ignore it.

- Have you considered the potential effects on your financial future? If your home is destroyed, are you prepared to walk away from your mortgage and ruin your credit?

- Do you have access to substantial emergency money? Consider getting a home equity line of credit before a disaster. After the disaster your home might be valueless.
- What forms of mitigation might minimize the effects of a disaster? Would the cost of special construction or modifications be less than the cost of an insurance policy?

When you decide to buy insurance, consider your existing insurance coverage, including the possibility of getting full replacement coverage. Check on local insurance requirements, state hurricane and earthquake insurance pools, and flood insurance from FEMA's National Flood Insurance Program. Flood insurance may be required for your mortgage if you live in a designated Special Flood Hazard area.

Insurance for Specific Disasters

Hurricane, tornado, and wind damage. This varies by state. In many areas your homeowner's policy already covers wind and hail damage, but hurricane-related flooding will probably not be covered. There are some state and private windstorm insurance pools. Ask your agent and the state office of emergency management.

Earthquake insurance is normally available at additional cost from your homeowner's insurance company. In some states where the risk is exceptionally high and private insurance may be prohibitively expensive, there may be a state earthquake insurance pool that offers a more reasonable rate. Again, check with the state office of emergency management.

Flood insurance can be a real pain. If it's not available for your homeowner's policy, try FEMA's National Flood Insurance Program (NFIP). The NFIP works in cooperation with private insurance companies. It basically subsidizes their losses.

A lot of people assume they are covered. In fact they may be covered only for certain types of flood damage or for none at all. There may be a waiting period for coverage after you've purchased your policy. If your insurance company can exploit any sort of loophole or nebulous wording in your policy, it will deny your claim. Some insurance companies will blacklist you if you even file a claim.

Insurance can be a conundrum. Shop around for the best coverage at the best price. Pay attention to horror stories about certain insurance companies. Make decisions based on sound research.

Keep current copies of policies with other important papers in a sturdy waterproof box.

11. Check Your Progress

Use this checklist to see if you've made any progress with personal and family preparedness:

- Contact your local emergency management office or the American Red Cross and learn about:
    - Likely disasters.
    - How you'll be warned.
    - How to prepare for each type of disaster.
- Complete your evacuation planning.
    - Make an escape plan for escape from each room and from the building.

- Consider escape plans for anyone in your family with special needs.
- Explain the escape and evacuation plans to the family or coworkers.

- Involve your family.
  - Discuss types of disasters in your area.
  - Explain how to prepare/respond.
  - Discuss what to do if told to evacuate.
  - Practice escape and evacuation plans.
- Devise a communications plan.
  - Pick two meeting places:
    - A location a safe distance from the house if there's a fire.
    - A location outside the area if the house area can't be reached.
  - Pick an out-of-state friend to be a "check-in person" for everyone to call.
  - Post emergency numbers, including the contact person's number, by every telephone.
- Prepare.
  - Show responsible family members where and how to shut off the utilities.
  - Install a smoke detector on each level of the home, especially near bedrooms. Test them monthly and change the batteries every six months (when daylight savings time changes).
  - Get on the internet or check with your local fire department to learn about fire hazards in the home and wildland fire hazards.
  - Make a disaster supplies kit. As a minimum, a three-day (72-hour) kit is recommended for the

> home and office, and a one-day (24-hour) kit for the car.
>
> ■ Learn first aid and CPR from the American Red Cross, the American Heart Association, the Emergency Care and Safety Institute.

- Meet with neighbors to:
  - ■ Plan how the neighborhood can work together after a disaster.
  - ■ Learn your neighbor's skills (medical, technical, logistic)
  - ■ Discuss how you will help neighbors with special needs (the elderly, disabled, non-English speaking, etc.).
  - ■ Plan for child care if parents can't get home during a disaster.

Chapter 3
Communications

1.   Accessing Public Information

There are literally tons and a gazillion super-megabytes of free information available regarding disaster planning, including mitigation, at countless agency offices and Web sites.

Immediately prior to and during a disaster, updated instructions and information may be somewhat more difficult to access. For most of the population, the best source of information will be radio and television. Listen to broadcast and cable radio and television stations for news and instructions, and follow the advice of local emergency officials.

Contrary to the Pollyanna belief of East Coast–based agencies like the CDC and FEMA, in many rural areas of the United States and other parts of the world, broadcast stations are far removed from their audience and listening to such a station may only provide vague general information that might be of little help. In the western U.S., most TV and radio stations serve and focus on the major metropolitan areas of the state and can be as far as 400 miles away from a listener on the other side of the same state. Residents in such rural areas will have to rely on local resources for updated information. It's a good idea to look at the local emergency plan and see how local authorities are planning to disseminate information to the public.

Printed media (newspapers) offer a secondary, belated source of information, and again focus on metropolitan areas.

The Emergency Alert System will provide limited information and instructions via the same radio and television stations. Also, the National Oceanic and Atmospheric Administration's National Weather Service radio system can be a source of all-hazards information. Many FRS, GMRS, and ham radios come configured for NOAA reception and may come with an encoder that automatically alerts you when information is being broadcast.

There are several excellent websites that provide current information on disaster events, including:

www.fema.gov—for information on domestic disasters.

www.reliefweb.int—for international information.

www.weather.gov and www.wunderground.com—for weather information.

2.   Communications Plans

Keep a battery or crank-operated radio in your home and workplace emergency kits, and include extra batteries.

Remember that family and business associates might be dispersed. Include in your plans how to contact each other.

At home and work, each person should have a copy of the contact list. The contact list should include whoever you've designated to check in with as well as the numbers for the doctor, hospital, office, schools, significant relatives, and emergency services. Post a list at home and workplace phones and put copies in the disaster supplies kits.

3. Communications Systems

Telecommunications systems can be categorized as primarily radio, data, or telephone systems, although cellular telephones are essentially radios.

Telephone Systems

Landlines

POTS (Plain Old Telephone Systems) are tied together through above or below ground hardwired systems. These traditional systems are powered through the phone line and will work during a power outage if the lines and stations are functioning. In an emergency local lines may be tied up, but long distance service might be available. Portable (not to be mistaken with cell) phones need electricity to work. Pay phones might work when other lines don't. Only use POTS lines if absolutely necessary during a disaster. 911 will need all available lines.

Cell phones

Cell phones rely on radio waves between the phone and a cellular tower. The radio channels can be overloaded, so call only when necessary. Also, cell service can be affected by power outages at the local servers or by destruction of relay and cell towers. Turn your cell off when not in use to conserve the battery. Cell phones can be charged in your car or with solar, crank, and emergency chargers.

Satellite phones

Satellite phones transmit through low-orbiting satellites. They don't work indoors. They are heavy and expensive, available for purchase or rental.

Function	Frequencies or Bands	Power	License requirement and Fee	Pros and Cons
CB Citizen's Band	27 MHz frequencies		No license required.	Short range. Emergency organizations include REACT.
FRS Family Radio Service	14 channels with 38 privacy tones.	Low (0.5 W)	No license requirement. No fee.	Short range. Mass marketed and very inexpensive.
GMRS General Mobile Radio Service	22 channels when combined with FRS.	1-5 watts	License required. Fee	Short range. FRS and GMRS radios may talk to each other on shared channels 1-7. Channels 15-22 are GMRS only. Mass marketed and very inexpensive.
MURS Multi-User Radio System	5 VHF channels	2 watts	No license required.	Short range. Defined by the FCC as a "private, two-way, short-distance voice or data communications service for personal or business activities of the general public."
Ham (Amateur) Radio	Extensive frequencies on multiple bands, HF, VHF, UHF, radio, TV, and data technology	1500 Watts	License required through examination.	Long distance communications possible when other systems are out. Emergency organizations include ARES and RACES.

Radio Systems

In the United States radio communications are regulated by the Federal Communications Commission, which assigns radio frequencies according to function.

There are several functions available to the public and non-governmental organizations (NGOs). Each function has its own frequencies and unique regulations.

Radio signals, like all electromagnetic radiation, usually travel in straight lines. However, at low frequencies (LF, below 3 MHz) diffraction effects allow them to partially follow the Earth's curvature, thus allowing AM radio signals in low-noise environments to be heard well after the transmitting antenna has dropped below the horizon. Additionally, frequencies between approximately 3 and 30 MHz (HF, or high frequency), can be reflected by the ionosphere, thus giving radio transmissions in this range a potentially global reach.

However, at higher frequencies (VHF and UHF), neither of these effects apply, and any obstruction between the transmitting and receiving antenna will block the signal. The ability to visually sight a transmitting antenna roughly corresponds with the ability to receive a signal from it. This propagation characteristic of high-frequency radio is called "line-of-sight."

In practice, the propagation characteristics of these radio bands vary substantially depending on the exact frequency and the strength of the transmitted signal (a function of both the transmitter and the antenna characteristics).

Low-powered transmitters (FRS, GMRS, MURS) can be blocked by a few trees, buildings, hills, or even heavy rain or snow. The presence of nearby objects not in the direct visual line of sight can also interfere with radio transmission.

Reflected radiation from the ground plane also acts to cancel out the direct signal. This effect can be reduced by raising the antennae further from the ground. The reduction in loss achieved is known as height gain, and it's the reason mobile and base antennas get better propagation than hand radios at the same wattage.

Getting Licensed

FRS, MURS, and CB do not require licensing. GMRS does require licensing, so if you're using a GMRS/FRS combination radio, you'll need a license. GMRS does not require an examination. In all countries amateur radio (ham) licensing requires an examination to prove knowledge of basic radio electronics and of communications rules and regulations. In return, hams get more frequencies (larger "bands") and can use a much wider variety of communication technologies at substantially higher power. In some countries a pre-test course is required.

For ham licensing information go to www.arrl.org.

For all licensing and regulations information, go to www.fcc.gov/uls/licenses.html.

Setting Up

Hand radios (walkie-talkies) don't require much setup. Take them out of the package. Put in some batteries and start communicating.

GMRS and FRS radios are available in any department store. Look for these features: full 14 channel FRS and 15

Left: GMRS/FRS radios in a charger. Middle: FM VHF
hand-held transceiver. Right: mobile VHF radio.

channel GMRS (note that 7 of the GMRS frequencies are
shared with FRS), water resistant or waterproof construction,
38 CTCSS codes (for privacy on whatever frequency you
choose), key lock, selectable call tones, programmable
channel scan, hands-free VOX (voice-operated-transmitting),
NOAA weather frequencies with alert. Get radios that use
conventional battery sizes so you can use disposable AA or
AAA batteries if your charger isn't available.

Mobile stations and base stations do take some
preparation. Have your mobile radio installed in your
vehicle by a professional. If you want to be able to use your

mobile as a base station, get some detailed advice or have it done professionally.

When installing a radio in your home or building, follow these steps for a comfortable and safe station:

- Give your radio its own desk.
- You will need access to the outside for the antenna and ground wires. Ground it as instructed in the installation manual.
- Give the radio proper clearance from walls for ventilation.
- Use earphones to minimize noise if you're sheltering with a group of people.
- Cover the radio when not in use to protect it from dust.

Making Contact

These are standard guidelines for two-way radio communications:

- Monitor the frequency or channel before transmitting.
- Plan your message before transmitting.
- Press the PTT (push-to-talk) button and very briefly pause.
- Hold the microphone two to three inches from the mouth.
- Identify the person(s) you're calling first.
- Acknowledge transmissions directed at you.
- Use plain English. No ten-codes or CB jargon.
- Do not use profanity.
- Reduce background noise as much as possible.

Data systems

For our purposes we'll define data as information, especially information in a form that can be used by a computer. It can include text, numbers, sounds and pictures. A single piece of information is called a datum. Data can be transmitted over radio waves or telephone systems. Devices used to transmit data include desktop and portable computers, PDAs, and fax machines. Fax machines use phone or radio service to send printed or illustrated data. E-mail is message data that can be transmitted over landline and wireless systems. E-mail has limited but important use in emergency and disaster communications, especially in the planning and recovery phases. It is relatively unreliable as a means of forecasting or warning due to the fact that e-mail isn't checked on a continuous basis. In addition, e-mail is a fourth-tier device, subject to failure of the lower tiers: power supply, landline or wireless system, server. Computer-accessed technology will not be available if power sources are knocked out or remote servers are damaged.

Communications technology screams ahead and what's new today is outdated in the blink of an eye. Amazing technologies are being incorporated, and the wise individual will try to keep up with the changes.

Primary and Backup Communications Systems

Some thought should be given to your continuity of communications. If your primary system goes down, how will you communicate with emergency responders, family members, and neighbors? Right now your primary means of communicating are your phones (POTS and cell) and your Internet. These are probably going to be overloaded or unavailable during a major disaster, leaving you with no way to communicate with the outside.

With some coordination and planning, an efficient and reliable backup communication system can be organized in your community. This type of system has been recommended by several individuals and agencies, and is probably the cheapest, most effective emergency backup system available for families and neighborhoods. It's also an effective system for small volunteer organizations looking for a cheap, reliable means of communicating in the field. In this system, every family or volunteer has an FRS radio. They are short range (half a mile). For every four or five families, one family is selected to be a GMRS/FRS radio coordinator. GMRS has a two-mile range and is compatible with FRS frequencies. For every four or five GMRS coordinators, one is selected to be a ham radio coordinator. Ham radios have a very long range in comparison to FRS and GMRS. The ham is responsible for communications outside the range of the FRS and GMRS radios.The beauty of a system like this is that it gives the public an alternative to trying to use an overloaded phone system, and it is organized in such a way that the radio communications do not interfere with each other. This is because there are so many channel and code combinations on FRS and GMRS, and the frequency bands for FRS, GMRS, and ham are different. Also, the short range of the FRS radios would ensure the FRS frequencies did not become overloaded with traffic from other neighborhoods. To minimize complications, neighborhoods would get together and agree on what frequencies are to be used for what purposes: evacuation, search and rescue, emergencies, or supply. Also, the local emergency response communications center would be included in the planning so they would know what frequency is their link to the GMRS or ham coordinators.

The system would look something like this:

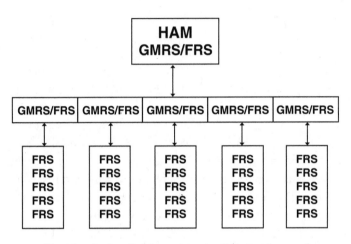

The drawback of this system is that it takes real coordination between neighbors—something that's hard to do these days.

Chapter 4
Power and Light

Storms and technological failures often take out our power. In a major disaster power could be lost for a week or more. When the power goes off, the heater blower stops running. The refrigerator stops. The freezer thaws. The ATM won't work. Electric pumps at the gas station won't work. Folks in rural areas lose the pumps that supply their water. People with medical conditions can face life-or-death situations waiting for lifesaving gadgets to kick back on. Worse, the TV goes off right in the middle of that lame reality show.

Of course, you can avoid these problems by investing in an emergency backup power system or by making arrangements with your rich neighbor to plug into his. Most of us will want our own. Since most of our appliances run on 120 volts AC, we basically have two options:

1. Buy a fuel-powered generator, or . . .
2. Use your car battery or a deep-cycle battery to power an inverter. An inverter is a device that changes 12-volt direct current from a battery into 120-volt AC.

The first step is to decide what you actually need and what you can afford. If you want to power a few fluorescent or LED lights, an electric blanket, and an emergency radio, you can get away with the inverter idea. If you want to keep your refrigerator going and run an electric heater and have plenty of light, you'll need a generator.

Electrical power is measured in watts. All appliances have an operating power. Devices that employ electrical motors or other devices that need an electrical kick also have what's called a *surge wattage,* which means extra watts are required to start the motor or device.

Common appliances and their typical power requirements	
Blow Dryer	900–1500 watts
CD/DVD player	35 watts
Clock radio	30–100 watts
Common light bulb	60 watts
Fan	75 watts (150 watts surge)
Color TV	300 watts (400 watts surge)
Coffee maker	650–1200 watts
Desktop computer system	400 watts (600 watts surge)
Electric blanket	80–100 watts
Electric heating pad	12–36 watts
Game box	100 watts
Microwave oven	750 watts (1500 watts surge)
Iron	1000 watts
Toaster	800–1500 watts
Furnace fan	750 watts (1500 watts surge)
Refrigerator	600–1200 watts
	(1200–2400 watts surge)
Vacuum cleaner	300–1100 watts
Satellite receiver	30 watts
Space heater	300–1100 watts
Stereo	30–100 watts
Washing machine	950 watts
Water cooler	120 watts
Well pump	2,400 watts
	(3,600 watts surge)
Electric water heater	4,500 watts
Whole-house AC or heat pump	15,000 watts (30,000 watts surge)

To figure out your power needs, add up the normal wattage figures for all the devices you might be using at the same time. Take the figures from this list or directly off the manufacturer's service tag on the device. If it doesn't give the wattage it will likely give the volts and amps. Multiply volts and amps together to get the watts. Add 20 percent to account for surge wattage. If a generator can't handle the surge wattage, the start up power will be unstable and can damage TVs and computers. Also, switching on a big-power device can cause the power to falter. Protect electronic devices with a good surge protector and/or an uninterruptible power supply (UPS).

Plan to stagger usage as much as possible. If you ensure your devices will not all be turned on at the same time, you can get along with a smaller, less expensive generator, or possibly even an inverter.

1.   Generators

Generators today are relatively cheap and are an easy way to get backup power. For instance, a reliable Coleman generator that produces 2500 watts and over 3100 surge can be purchased for under $500 and will provide 10 hours of power on a 3 gallon tank of gas. Propane- and diesel-burning generators are also available. When the diesel fuel is gone, diesel generators can burn filtered vegetable oils or an oil and diesel mix, but it will eventually clog the fuel injectors.

Generators do have some distinct disadvantages. They produce toxic fumes and must be run outside away from windows and doors. They tend to break down frequently. They make a lot of noise (some are far better than others in

For long-term backup power a heavy-duty generator will outlast a light recreational generator, and a larger fuel tank like this one will let the generator run longer before refueling is required.

that regard). And they require large quantities of fuel, which must be stored somewhere where it won't be a hazard. Gasoline has a short shelf-life, even with stabilizers added. I have used gasoline that was stored for over a year without chemical stabilizers. Fuel storage should be rotated on a frequent basis.

2. Inverters

Using an inverter for emergency power is an excellent choice if your power needs are limited. Inverters are devices that change 12-volt battery power to 120-volt AC power. There are two general types of power inverters: true-sine wave and modified-sine wave (square wave). True-sine wave inverters produce power that is either identical to or sometimes slightly better than power from the power company. The power wave when viewed through an oscilloscope is a smooth sine wave.

Modified-sine wave and square wave inverters are the most common types of power inverters on the market. Modified-sine wave power inverters produce a power wave that is sufficient for most devices.

Before you purchase an inverter you will want to take a piece of paper and a pen and write down all of the appliances that you feel are necessary to have during a power outage, *then figure out their total operating wattage.*

Smaller watt totals (say, under 300 watts) can get along with an inexpensive small inverter that costs under $50. Inverters in that range can be plugged directly into the car's lighter socket. Depending on your car battery's reserve capacity rating, a good battery will give you 150 watts for an hour or two without the engine running. If you're only using 20 watts, the battery could last 20 hours. But don't let it go that far. Run the engine often to recharge the battery. To run a larger inverter (over 300 watts), you'll want to connect it directly to the car's battery with the cables provided, and you will need to run the engine continuously. A car's alternator can only supply about 700 watts maximum. It's best to purchase an inverter well under that wattage if you don't want to start blowing car fuses. However, if more power is needed, it's feasible to run inverters of 1,750 watts or more off of multiple batteries in parallel or deep-cycle batteries (these are different from your car battery). But at that

Left: a 750 watt (1500 peak watt) inverter that clamps to
battery posts. Right: a 150 watt (300 peak watt) inverter
that plugs into a car lighter socket.

point it would probably be just as cheap and easier to buy
a generator.

When you hook a big inverter up to your vehicle battery,
you will want to try to keep the inverter close to the battery,
and out of the rain or snow.

It makes sense to have both generator and inverter
backup capabilities. They can be staggered to provide
different wattages at peak and low usage periods.

3.   How to Wire Your House or Building

The easiest way by far to bring electricity in from the generator
or inverter is to run in extension cords. You can run cords
in for individual appliances, or you can run in a cord with
multiple outlets. The disadvantage to multiple outlets is that

you will have to closely police them so the group is not plugging in at the wrong time and overloading the system.

If you have super-high wattage or voltage requirements (for instance, if you want to run your furnace blower or a well pump) or are dependent on 240-volts for major appliances, you're going to need a big expensive generator, and you'll want to consider having the generator wired into your circuit panel so all the outlets in the house have power. If you decide to do that, you must understand several important things:

- Do not try to wire the panel yourself unless you are an electrician. You've spent gobs of money on that big generator, spend a few more dollars on proper installation.
- Be sure to have the generator grounded according to the instructions in the operator's manual.

Always cut your house off from the power grid before starting the generator. If you don't, your precious electricity will be transmitted out of your home and it could electrocute anyone working on the line. A positive interlock system installed by an electrician will ensure that the house main breaker is cut off when the generator's breaker turns on.

4.   Other Systems

Any system that supplies the needs of an entire home or building is going to cost a lot of money to construct. Solar, wind, and water systems are extremely expensive to build and only work when it's sunny, windy, or the water's flowing. If you're going to rely on solar systems for large power needs, you're going to need several hundred watts of solar power to keep the batteries charged, or run a generator to do it. The big concern with complicated systems is this: if you don't take care of it, it will not work when you need it and you will have wasted your money.

If you don't know anything about electricity, don't try installing electrical systems of any kind. You can burn down your house, fry your car, electrocute your children and the repairman, cause an explosion, cause battery acid burns and toxic gas exposures, and fibrillate your own heart. Be sensible.

5. In the Event of a Blackout

- Before you rig up your alternative power sources, turn off or unplug all devices to avoid a damaging surge when the power comes back on.
- Maintain your refrigerator/freezer protocol
- If appliances get wet, turn of the power main, unplug the appliances, and allow them to dry out before plugging them in again.

Generator Safety

Take the following precautions when using a generator:

- Don't plug your generator into a regular household outlet. You can kill somebody outside your building and not even know it.
- Don't overload the generator. Add up the watts of your appliances and leave some room for surge voltages.
- Don't use a generator indoors or in an attached garage. Place it where carbon monoxide will not drift into your building. Operate it outdoors in a well

ventilated area away from windows and airvents and protected from the weather.

- Use proper power cords that are heavy duty and rated for use outdoors. Cords are a trip hazard. Tape them in place, but do not put them under the carpet where they can overheat.
- Make sure your generator is properly grounded, according to the instructions in the operator's manual.
- Do not store fuel indoors
- Do not refuel while the generator is still running or when it is still hot.
- All equipment powered by the generator should be tunred off before shutting the generator down.
- The generator will get hot. Don't get burned.
- Keep children away from the generator.

Batteries

Some battery basics:

- For convenience, all your battery operated appliances and equipment should use the same battery size.
- Replaced stored batteries annually. If batteries are stored in a dry place at room temperature—not in a refrigerator or freezer—their shelf life can be as long as three years or more.
- Stick to disposable alkaline batteries or to rechargeable NiMH batteries. Lithium batteries are expensive. Alkaline batteries are cheaper than lithium, but lithium batteries work better at colder temperatures. NiCad batteries have two-thirds the life of alkaline batteries and can be recharged 500 times. Rechargeable NiMH batteries have four-fifths the life of alkaline batteries.

You can get rechargeable alkaline batteries, but they have only half the life of disposable alkalines and they can only be recharged about 25 times.

- Chargers can be run off a generator, an inverter, and solar panels.

- If you are not going to use your flashlight or other device, remove the batteries to prevent damage from leaking battery acid.

6.   Alternate Light Sources

Oil lamps, candles, kerosene lamps, and mantle lamps: Avoid them. They're a fire hazard. Kerosene oil lamps provide some limited heat as well as light. They're brighter than a candle but usually barely bright enough to read by. FYI, "lamp oil" is #1-grade kerosene.

If you're using these lamps, you must ventilate. Keep extra wicks in your disaster kit. Be careful where you place a lit lamp. It can get extremely hot above the lamp chimney. Glass can shatter. Metal-frame lamps are safer than glass-frame lamps.

Mantles are very fragile when ignited and require frequent replacement. The light of a mantle lamp is intense. Liquid fuel (white gas) requires pumping to pressurize the tank. Do not use unleaded gasoline in these lamps, unless the lantern is designed for it. Otherwise, the additives in the fuel will cause clogging.

Camp lamps with screw-in propane cannisters are the most convenient of these types of lamps. There's no pumping and no spilling. Their disadvantage is the fire hazard and the fact that they are less efficient at cold temperatures.

Light sticks: These provide cool low-level light for several hours. The light is non-directional, but can be rigged with a foil reflector to function as a flashlight.

Flashlights and headlamps: The normal iridescent bulbs that used to be in all our flashlights waste most of their energy as heat. Fluorescent and LED lights are far more power-efficient. LED bulbs last over 10,000 hours and are shock and cold-resistant. Fluorescent bulbs last ten times longer than iridescent bulbs but are not bright at cold temperatures. LED flashlights using groups of three to nine bulbs will work six times as long as their equivalent iridescent bulbs on the same batteries. LED lights now come in a big assortment of flashlights and headlights, using batteries, cranks, or solar power. Multi-LED touchlamps for your home or car cost around $10.

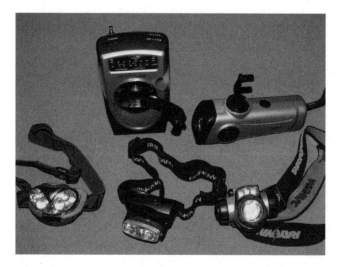

LED headlamps, flashlights, lamps.

Chapter 5
Emergency Heating and Cooling

1.   Emergency Heating

"Many are cold, but few are frozen."

So the power and gas go off and you're faced with a heating crisis, and all sorts of bad things can result from it. Your house pipes can freeze, causing structural damage. Your drinking water and food can freeze, leaving you struggling to avoid dehydration. Probably the biggest hazards are the alternative heating sources that are often used. In a real disaster the potential for an emergency is increased because fire and emergency medical services are already overwhelmed and may not be able to respond. For this reason, safety must your primary concern when determining alternative forms of heat. Not a lot of people have frozen to death in their homes, but plenty have died from fires, smoke inhalation, and carbon monoxide.

Look at what you can do to your home to mitigate the problem. Caulking and weather-stripping doors and windows, plugging holes and air conditioning vents, applying a layer of plastic or an extra pane over windows, installing insulating curtains. Have your fireplace or wood stove checked by a professional and get your chimney swept. Install battery-operated smoke alarms on every level of the building and check them frequently. Consider installing a battery-operated carbon monoxide detector.

During a heating emergency your first step is to put on some warm clothes, then take the following steps:

- Find or improvise a heat source
- Obtain fuel
- Select an area or a room to be heated
- Set up and operate the emergency heater
- Deal with related problems—appraise for safety and make immediate changes

In the planning stages you'll need to define the scope of the problem. In other words, how cold can it get, and how much will you and your home be affected? Even if your furnace burns fuel, how will it distribute the heat? Fuel injectors, igniters, circulator pumps, motorized stokers, and most thermostats require electricity, and most coal, oil, and water heating systems are dependent on getting power.

As you're making your family plan or business plan, discuss the topic of alternative heating sources with your family members or business associates. What and where are they? How do you use them? How will you keep pipes from freezing? Consider your options. Could you operate the normal heating system by making minor modifications or operating it manually? With the right parts from your local gas supplier, could your natural gas appliances be modified to run off of bottled gas? If your oven burns fuel, could you just simply turn it on and open the oven door? Are there other heating devices on the location that can be used, e.g., fireplace, wood stove, gas stove or oven, oil stove, space heater, camp stove, portable electric heater? Make a list of the fuels at or near your location. Can they be used in any of the alternative devices you thought of? Potential alternative fuels might include newspapers and magazines rolled tightly into log-sized bundles, dried weeds, firewood and lumber scraps, coal, charcoal, oil, kerosene, gas, camp-stove fuel, starter fluid, alcohol, gasoline, motor oil, fat and grease, and even wood furniture and fixtures. Finally, ask yourself how much heat the alternative sources can supply (enough for several rooms? or a single room?), and for how long.

If you can't figure out a way to modify and operate your normal heating system or other devices you already have to produce adequate heat, it's time to purchase or make another device that can. It may be as simple as getting a generator to run your heat pump. Or you might choose to purchase electric, gas, or kerosene space heaters or a wood-burning stove. Just remember . . .

Any heater that burns fuel must be vented to the outside in order to eliminate smoke and toxic fumes and to obtain oxygen for combustion. Make modifications and preparations ahead of time by having a professional set up a stovepipe or vent and flue.

2. Conserving Heat

During an actual heating emergency, your fist concern should be conserving body heat. Here are some key points regarding heat conservation:

- Eat enough food and drink enough water. Dehydration and low blood sugar accelerate the onset and progress of hypothermia.
- Wear winter clothing, preferably many insulating layers rather than one huge bulky layer. Layers can be added or removed to adjust to the temperature.
- Additional insulation can be provided by sleeping bags, tarps, blankets, curtains, rugs, big towels, cardboard, or newspapers.

- Consider personal heating devices that would have a small demand on inverters or generators. These include electric blankets and heating pads.

- Huddle together, everyone in the same room. Consider huddling with your neighbors for additional heat.

- In your home, bed will be the warmest place. You can share body heat there with other family members and pile the bed high with whatever insulation you find.

- Sleeping in a tent pitched indoors will conserve body heat at night. If you have no indoors, a tent might be all you have, and you will be glad you have it.

- If you have no shelter, find some. A community emergency shelter will be heated.

- The smaller the space you heat, the easier it will be to heat it and maintain the heat. Choose one or two rooms. If you have a fuel-burning stove or a fireplace, the choice has been made for you. If you're going to use a portable heater, choose a room on the warmer side of the building, ideally away from prevailing winds but exposed to the sun. Choose a well-insulated room with few windows over a poorly insulated room with big windows. Interior bathrooms are well suited for this. A basement may actually be warmer than the rest of the house because it may conduct heat from the ground. Insulate windows and openings, and partition with cardboard, curtains, or plywood if necessary. Close the door and block other openings to prevents unwanted drafts, but remember that if you're using a fuel-burning stove or heater, you'll need a chimney vent or flue or you'll need to provide a cross-draft for ventilation.

- Bring your stored water into that same room to keep it from freezing, or run a heating pad into the storage area from your inverter or generator.

If it's already frozen, bring it in to passively thaw. Actively melting ice or snow for water is a waste of precious fuel.

- If your house has no heater and you have a trailer or camper with one, move into it.
- As a last resort, get into your car and use the heater. This is risky, and you should carefully ventilate the cab to prevent carbon monoxide poisoning.

3.   Safety

- The very, very last resort is using improvised heaters like charcoal grills and gas ovens. These are very risky. Charcoal will produce copious carbon monoxide. Gas ovens are an asphyxiation and explosion hazard. If you use them be prepared to provide plenty of ventilation to outside air. Better to be cold than dead.

- ***If you're using a catalytic heater, a fuel-burning heater that provides heat with no flame, or any unvented fuel-burning heater, provide adequate ventilation. Keep a nearby window open at least one inch whenever the heater is used, but close it when the heater is not being used to prevent heat loss. Even better, provide cross-ventilation by opening a window one inch on each side of the room.***

- Turn fuel-burning space heaters off before you go to bed. ***Never sleep in a fuel-heated room with no ventilation.*** Having an extra battery-operated carbon monoxide detector for the sleeping room is a good idea.

- If you plan to use unvented gas or kerosene heaters, the following applies:

- Read the manufacturer's instructions carefully.
- Use space heaters that are certified to meet safety standards by the Underwriters' Laboratories (UL) or the American Gas Association laboratories.
- Use space heaters that have an oxygen depletion valve so it shuts off if there's a lack of good air or there's excessive carbon dioxide.
- Use only gas heaters that have a pilot safety valve. If the pilot goes off, it will shut off the gas.
- Have the heater inspected before you store it. If you use it, have it inspected annually.
- Use only the fuel for which the appliance was designed.
- In a kerosene heater, use only clear white water-free IK kerosene.
- Refuel heaters outside with the fuel valve closed and after the device has cooled. Never attempt to refuel while the stove is still lit. Fill only as directed in the owner's manual.

Keep flammable materials away from vents and stovepipes. Keep portable heaters several feet away from furniture and other flammables.

- If you're using wood or coal burning stoves, be careful with the ashes. Empty them in a covered metal container and store them outside away from combustibles. Do NOT attempt to vacuum up dry ashes.
- Assign someone to fire watch whenever open-flame cooking and heating are in progress.

- Set up your firefighting items near your heating and cooking devices. If you don't have a dry-powder extinguisher, keep a bucket of sand, salt, baking soda, or water to smother and cool the fire (the water will not work on liquid fuels and may actually spread the fire). A heavy blanket can be used to smother a small fire. Make sure the family or group understands the evacuation plan and at least two ways out of the building.

- If you have neighbors with special needs, do a courtesy check to ensure they are safe.

3.   Storing Emergency Fuel

Store enough for several days. If your kit is a three-day kit, store enough for three days. If it's a two-week kit, store enough for two weeks. Fuels should be stored in a safe place away from the house or building, such as a garage or shed. Rotate the fuel by occasionally using it to fill your car or to fuel a campout, but always replace it immediately.

During the emergency, store the fuel where it's easily accessible, but do NOT store flammable or highly combustible fuels like gas and kerosene in the heated area.

Find out if there are community stockpiles of emergency fuel, and where community plans have designated emergency shelters.

4.   Dealing with Frozen Pipes

Drain pipes and containers that will not be getting heat. This should include house plumbing, toilet tanks and bowls, bathtub, dish and clothes washers and their hoses, the hot water heater tank, and the furnace boiler in any room where the temperature drops below 35 degrees. Cover undrained pipes with whatever insulation you can spare. Consider heating vulnerable pipes with a heating pad (only 12 to 36 watts each) from your inverter or generator. If the water supply is intact and the main valve open, try running a trickle of water from a faucet or two to keep the water circulating, which helps prevent it from freezing.

To flush toilets, use a bucket of water that is not fit for drinking or cooking (*see* Chapter 6: Water). Flush only as often as it's necessary in order to prevent the system from clogging or freezing.

5.   Emergency Cooling

When it's so hot that "cows give evaporated milk."

So the power goes off during a heat wave and you're faced with a cooling crisis, and all sorts of bad things occur because of it. The fans and air conditioners stop. Your ice melts, your food rots. Everybody gets dehydrated and cranky or truly sick. Like heating emergencies, cooling emergencies can be a real threat. Heat is especially hard on the very young or very old, and anyone with chronic health problems. See chapter 9 for first aid information for heat and cold illnesses.

There are plenty of things to do to limit the effects of heat:

- Prepare for the heat. In the evening open the windows and turn on the fans for cross-ventilation. That will cool the house down. When the sun comes up in the morning, shut all the windows and doors, close the curtains, and leave them shut and closed all day until cooler evening. Then open things up again.

- Drink plenty of water, even if you're not thirsty, and even if it's humid. Dehydration will speed the effects of heat illnesses. Alcohol will dehydrate you, and caffeinated, carbonated, and heavily sugared drinks like lemonade are not efficient hydrators. If it's real hot, drink the coolest water you can find. Be aware that it IS possible to overhydrate. On a hot day with moderate physical activity an adult will go through about a gallon. Too much more than that can cause a condition called hyponatremia, with symptoms similar to those of heat injuries.

- Sports drinks can be beneficial in replacing electrolytes that you have sweated off. Avoid salt tablets unless a doctor tells you otherwise.

- Avoid strenuous activity, and work during the coolest parts of the day (early morning).

- Stay inside, or at least avoid direct sunlight and stay in shaded areas. Outside, wear lightweight, loose-fitting, long-sleeved clothing. A hat with a large brim helps protect against the sun.

- If possible, keep the air moving. Put a fan in an upstairs window to blow off the heat in the upper levels. A fan in a lower window will help create a heat-reducing cross-draft.

- Turn off any sources of heat, including lights and computers. Keep the stove off. Eat foods that don't require cooking.

- Eat frequent small meals and avoid high protein foods.

- Move to the lowest level of the building (probably the basement). Cold air is more dense and sinks to lower levels. Also, lower levels might stay cooler because of the colder ground it conducts from.

- Wet your wrists with cold or ice water.

- If you're sweating, use it to your advantage. Stand in a breeze or in front of a fan. When water evaporates, it absorbs heat, drawing it away from the body.

- Get in a tub of water or take a shower if it doesn't deplete precious water supplies. Sit with your hands or feet in a basin of cold water.

- Fill a glass with ice and blow into it and let your face catch the cool air that comes out.

- Take off your shoes and hats. The head and feet have a big role in regulating body temperature.

- If you can't keep up with the heat, go to a community shelter where it's likely to be cooled.

- Turn yourself into a human swamp cooler. If you live in a dry climate, one of these techniques can cool you off considerably:

  - Use a squirt bottle to saturate the sleeves of your shirt or the legs of your pants. Evaporation will cool the arms and legs.

  - Put on a dripping wet T-shirt. Be prepared for strange looks, but at least you'll be cooled off for an hour or so.

  - Put a wet towel on the back of the neck or top of the head.

  - Consider wearing a "gutra," the large white scarf made of thin breathable material and worn by Arabian men. Make your own out of whatever thin material you can find. Soak it with water and plant yourself in a breeze. Reap the benefits. The author actually tested the cooling efficiency of wet gutras while doing remote backcountry projects in Arabia. The temperature difference between unshaded air outside the gutra and air around the face beneath the gutra is significant.

- Run a fan over an ice chest. It will melt precious ice, but it can provide localized relief for a couple of hours.

- Consider purchasing an expensive portable single-room air conditioner, with the understanding that running it will require about 700 watts or more to cool about 300 square feet. That means you'll need a generator to run it if the power's off.

Portable air coolers (swamp coolers) can be found for less than $100 and can run on less than 100 watts from an inverter. Unfortunately they're only effective in dry climates.

The bottom line is that with some basic knowledge and preparation you can survive a disastrous heat wave. Sufficient water is a key, both for hydration and body-cooling.

Chapter 6
Water

The importance of proper hydration can't be over-emphasized. Active adults need at least two liters of water or the equivalent per day, more in extreme conditions, and dehydration can easily become life-threatening within a few days. In a major disaster you can expect to lose your normal sources of water due to the loss of power to pumps, structural damage, or contamination. If you think there's a chance your water sources will be cut off, fill the tub and other clean containers as soon as possible and then shut off the main supply to protect the water that remains in the house.

Here are some rules of thumb regarding water in disaster situations:

- Store a minimum of three days of water, at a gallon per day per person. Add more if you have children, nursing mothers, chronically ill family members, if your group will be very physically active, or if your area experiences excessively hot or cold weather.

- Drink only the water you know is safe, and NEVER drink floodwater.

- Potentially contaminated water can be used after it has been purified or treated properly as long as there's no lingering chemical contamination.

- Reduce your water and food requirements by keeping physical activity to a minimum.

- Don't ration water unless told to do so by the authorities.

- Caffeine, alcohol, and dehydrated and freeze-dried foods do not contribute to hydration. Use these drinks and foods cautiously in moderation and not as a substitution for water or other fluids.

The primary safe sources of water for consumption will be commercially bottled water or tap water that's been stored beforehand with your disaster kit.

Commercially bottled water should be kept sealed until it's used. Try to comply with use-by dates but don't just toss it out if it's past its date.

Tap water can be stored in food-grade water storage containers that can be purchased at preparedness and outdoor sports stores or in sanitized two-liter or gallon soda or water bottles. Don't use milk or juice bottles, because the odor and taste can carry over, and unless they're thoroughly sanitized, they can culture bacteria. Use plastic instead of glass containers to avoid getting your water containers shattered. Also, consider mobility. If you need to evacuate your home, a 20-gallon container is going to weigh 160 pounds and won't fit in your backpack. Smaller containers can be divided among the group and will be easier to handle.

To clean and sanitize containers for water storage, follow these steps:

- Clean the container with a dash of dishwashing soap and lots of hot water, then rinse thoroughly several times.
- Drop a teaspoon (5 ml) per quart of unscented liquid bleach (3 to 6 percent sodium hypochlorite) into the container, replace the lid loosely, shake the container to completely cover all surfaces, then hold the bottle upside down to make sure the remaining bleach coats

Large commercial water containers are available from stores handling emergency preparedness supplies. Above: a seven-gallon container that integrates a water filter in the spigot, along with a hand-operated water filter. Water containers should be food-grade, made of materials that are shatterproof and will not off-gas chemical vapors into the water. On the bottom of the container there will be a triangle with a number in it. Generally the safer choices for food and water storage have a triangle with number 1, 2, 4, or 5.

the neck of the bottle and the inside of the screw cap. Rinse with water that you know is clean, preferably water that has been purified and treated.

- Fill the bottle with water to the top. If the water is treated already (tap water from an uncontaminated water line, or water purified and treated by you), then screw on the cap tightly and store the container in a cool, dark place. If the water is untreated, before putting it in the bottle perform the purification or treatment processes discussed later.
- Replace stored water every six months.

Of course, everything is amazingly simpler if you just go down to the local discount store and purchase water in plastic one- or three-gallon jugs. They are cheap and easily replaced.

Once you have lost your main source of water and you have started using your stored water, you should be searching for alternative sources for future use. How do you determine which sources are safe?

First, make it perfectly clear to your group that the stored drinking water is only for consumption, not for flushing toilets and washing clothes. Use other questionable water resources for those purposes.

The following sources can be considered safe for drinking and cooking if no contamination has occurred prior to shutting off the main water valve:

- Remaining pipe water.
- Toilet tankwater, if not treated with cleaning or deodorizing chemicals. A few drops of bleach will make skeptics more comfortable.
- Water from undamaged hot-water heater tanks.

The following sources can be used if properly purified or treated:

- Water from wells and cisterns
- Rainwater and water from streams, rivers, ponds, and natural springs
- Salt water

Water from radiators, swimming pools, and hot tubs should be considered unsafe and used for flushing toilets and washing clothes.

To use the water remaining in house pipes, open the highest faucet in the house or building and get water from the lower faucets. To get the water out of the main hot water heater tank, shut off the electricity and gas, close the cold water intake valve, and drain the water from the hot water valve. Refill the tank before turning the electricity or gas back on.

1. Contamination

Disasters can contaminate local water resources. Water can be contaminated with industrial pollutants (chemicals), but the contamination is usually by microorganisms (bacteria, viruses, protozoa, helminthes) from sewage, causing diseases such as cholera, typhoid, dysentery, and hepatitis. Once many of these diseases have started, they are rapidly spread through bad water consumption and oral-fecal contamination (for example, the germs from scratching your butt getting left on the doorknobs you handle).

Simple hygiene—washing the hands and cleaning utensils—can prevent gastrointestinal diseases. Use warm soapy water for cleaning hands, especially after urination and defecation. Alcohol-based hand sanitizers are good to have around, but remember that they are only effective when there is no visible dirt on your hands. So wash with soap and water anyway.

Keep cooking and eating utensils clean and as sanitized as possible. Do not use contaminated, untreated water to wash or rinse utensils. The rumor that all pathogens will die when the dishes dry is completely false. Consider storing a week's worth of paper plates, disposable cups, and disposable utensils with your disaster supplies.

2.   Purification and Treatment

Gastrointestinal illness from bad water is a major cause of death from hypovolemia and diarrhea during disasters. The goal of purifying and treating water is to reduce the pathogens ("germs") to an acceptably low risk of causing illness. Always keep in mind that judging water by taste, appearance, and source are not always reliable methods.

The most common ways of treating and purifying water are simple:

- Distillation (see below).
- Boiling for a few minutes (longer at higher altitudes, where the boiling point is lower than at sea level).
- Chemical treatment from chemical purification tablets or household liquid chlorine (3 to 6 percent unscented sodium hypochlorite) at four to eight drops per quart. Shake and stir, then let sit for 30 minutes.
- Water filters, which vary greatly in their effectiveness.
- Solar disinfection (SODIS).

Steps in Water Purification

STEP 1: Screening

Screening removes the largest contaminants.

Fill a container by dripping or pouring water through a cloth, bandana, handkerchief, coffee filter, T-shirt, or fine strainer.

STEP 2: Standing

Allow the water to remain completely still for an hour. Clean off the floaters and then pour off the water into another container to leave the sediment behind.

STEP 3: Flocculating

This is an optional process that removes fine suspended particles.

Add a pinch of alum or baking powder per gallon. Stir gently for five minutes. This promotes agglomeration of small particles to form a precipitate. Let it stand for a few minutes then pour off the clean water or filter through a coffee filter.

STEP 4: Disinfection

This step is accomplished by using one or more of the following methods:

Heat

Most GI pathogens are easily destroyed by heat. The effectiveness of heat depends on the temperature and the exposure time. Lower temperatures can be effective at longer exposure times.

It's risky to estimate temperatures, so use the boiling point as the target temperature. At that temperature, disinfection has already occurred by the time the water boils. At altitudes over 6500 feet (2000m) the CDC recommends boiling for three minutes.

When heating the water, cover the pot to preserve and retain heat. A rolling boil washes the germs on the inside back down into the water where they are killed.

Filters

Filters screen out bacteria, protozoa, helminthes and their cysts and eggs if they filter down to the 0.2 micron range. Most filters are not reliable against viruses less than 0.1 micron in size. Filters clog over time, and operating a clogged filter can actually force pathogens through. Filters impregnated with iodine or bactericidal crystals are of questionable efficiency. When unclear about the efficiency of a filter system, use other methods of disinfection as a final step.

• *(cont'd.)*

Steps in water purification

Chemicals (Halogenation)

Halogenation uses chemicals like iodine and chlorine bleach. These chemicals are effective against viruses and bacteria, but their efficiency against helminthes and protozoa and their eggs varies. Cryptosporidium, a parasite commonly found in lakes and rivers, especially when the water is contaminated with sewage and animal waste, is resistant to halogenation.

The efficiency of halogen depends on the concentration, the length of exposure, the temperature of the water, pH, and the presence of contaminants. Chlorine bleach is the most sensitive to these factors and is less suited for cold water. In these conditions halogens require increased time and increased concentration. Be sure to strain it first. Particulates deactivate halogen.

The standard dose of chlorine bleach (6 percent) for disinfection is four drops to a quart of water, left to sit for 30 minutes at room temperature. Increase (up to double) that amount if the water is dirty, and increase the setting time to an hour.

The bad taste left by halogens can be minimized by adding some ascorbic acid (vitamin C) or flavored drink mixes after the disinfection process is completed. A pinch of activated charcoal can reduce the chemical load.

Note that with iodine some changes in thyroid function have been noted. Avoid using high doses of iodine (e.g., water purification tablets) for more than a month or two. Iodine should NOT be used to disinfect water consumed by individuals with known thyroid disease, pregnancy, or iodine allergies.

Other methods

Other methods of purifying water include UV radiation and chlorine dioxide.

UV disinfection using special lamps is effective against even stubborn cysts. The problem with UV is that the lamps require a lot of energy to run, and particulates can shield the pathogens. In a worst case scenario it would be possible to achieve adequate disinfection by using a process called sodis (solar disinfection). Sodis is performed by simply filling a one- or two-liter plastic water bottle with screened or filtered water and laying it on its side outside on a light-colored reflective surface like cement, tile, or metal. If the sun's out, the UV radiation from the sun will disinfect the water within six hours. If it's cloudy, leave the bottle out for at least two days. The process sounds questionable to Westerners, but it's being used with success in many third world countries. Any clear plastic or glass bottle can be used, but the best plastic bottles are those that have a faint blue tinge.

Chlorine dioxide comes in liquid and tablet options. It reacts less with pollutants than chlorine bleach and is effective against a wider range of pH. It also has less offensive taste than halogens, and is effective against cryptosporidium.

Steps in water purification

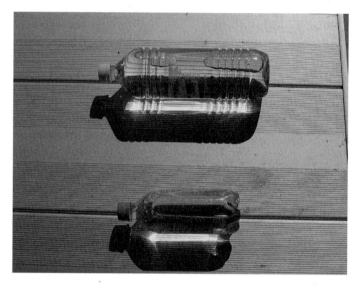

Sodis: Filter the water through a coffee filter or fine
screen first. Place it on a shiny metal or white surface.
UV radiation from direct sunlight will disinfect the water
within six hours.

Before doing any of this it's important to remove large
particles that can interfere with the purification process and
make drinking unpleasant.

If you're serious about getting the best water possible,
the purification and treatment process is necessarily a
detailed, multi-step procedure involving screening, standing,
flocculation (optional), and disinfection.

Distillation

Distillation is a slow process that is gadget-intensive, but it
will remove microbes that resist other methods, and heavy

	Heat	Filtration	Halogenation	Sodis	Distillation
Bacteria	Fair	Fair	Good	Good	Good
Viruses	Fair	Poor	Fair	Good	Good
Protozoa and Cysts	Good	Good	Fair	Good	Good
Helminths and oocysts	Good	Good	Poor	Poor	Good
Chemicals including heavy metals and salts	None	Fair	None	None	Good

Effectiveness of different methods of purification.

metals, salts, and most other chemicals. It is the ONLY way you'll be able to prepare saltwater for consumption. It involves boiling water and then collecting the vapor that condenses back to water. Distilled water is popular, and countertop distillers are available for under a hundred dollars. The problem is they require electricity, which you might not have unless you have an alternative power source. There are also some camp-stove distillers on the market. Their drawback is the fuel requirement. To distill without one of these devices, a Red Cross site recommends the following method: fill a pot halfway with water. Tie a cup to the handle on the pot's lid so that the cup will hang right-side-up when the lid is upside-down (make sure the cup is not dangling into the water) and boil the water for 20 minutes. The water that drips from the lid into the cup is distilled.

Chapter 7
Food and Nutrition

During and right after a disaster, it's important to eat enough to maintain your strength and alertness. When we get hypoglycemic one of the first symptoms is a decrease in mental clarity. It's OK to ration food if you think the disaster will be prolonged. But eat at least one large well-balanced meal each day. It's NOT OK to ration water. The body can function adequately for extended periods with reduced food, but skimping on water or fluids will quickly lead to dehydration. Drink a minimum of two quarts per day to insure you're getting enough. Take in enough calories to enable you to do any necessary work. If you don't have the food to keep up with the work, then reduce the workload first, then the food consumption if necessary. Include vitamin, mineral, and protein supplements in your food storage.

The ideal food supply for a disaster situation will be relatively compact and lightweight (for portability), requiring no refrigeration and minimum cooking (which requires electricity and/or fuel), and requiring little water.

But let's back up and look at those two technological pieces: refrigeration and cooking. In a major disaster our electricity will be cut off. It could be days or weeks before it's restored. Obviously you'll need to eat the perishables first, and that's going to require some cooking. You'll need to take some steps to keep the perishables as long as they can keep, and to provide yourself with an alternative means of cooking.

1.   Emergency Refrigeration

After the power fails, avoid opening the refrigerator or freezer. An unopened fridge will remain adequately cold for about two hours. Insulating the fridge or freezer with blankets will retard the escape of cold, but be careful not to block vents.

Additional time can be gained by transferring ice blocks from the freezer to the refrigerator, and by putting dry ice in the freezer. The transfer should take seconds, not minutes, or the benefits will be lost. Open the refrigerator and freezer doors only as long as it takes to quickly move the ice.

The amount of dead air space in a fridge or freezer affects the time it will maintain an acceptable temperature. Fuller is better. Solid ice blocks and cold water bottles displace harmful warm air. A fridge full of ice blocks or ice water will last much longer than a fridge that is half full.

If the power is still on, or if you have a warning period before an event, turn the temperature to maximum cold in both the fridge and the freezer and start making ice blocks.

If coolers are used, put ice in the cooler first to pre-cool it then quickly transfer the food. Dead air in a cooler has the same effect it has in the fridge. Use a smaller cooler to avoid dead air. Store the cooler in a cool shaded location and insulate it with a blanket. Don't drain the meltwater unless absolutely necessary. Cold water stays colder longer than cold air.

Dry ice is frozen carbon dioxide. It has several times the cooling energy of water ice per equivalent volume. It's so cold that it can actually burn the skin. It sublimes instead of freezing: five pounds will sublime within a day in a cooler. Dry ice can be used to extend the life of regular ice. Unfortunately, dry ice will be in extremely short supply after a disaster. If you're going to need it, you'd better make arrangements with your supplier (usually a large supermarket) beforehand.

Once the power has gone off, you need to start "triaging" your food supply. Eat perishable items from the refrigerator first. Eat or toss out meat, poultry, seafood, dairy, and all cooked foods if they've been in a closed fridge without power, with a temperature greater than 40 degrees, longer than four hours. A thermometer for the fridge is a good idea, but do NOT open the fridge to check the temperature. Plan to check the temperature only when the fridge is opened to obtain food. If you have your refrigerator packed with ice blocks, the food should be good until the ice blocks are melted as long as the interior temperature stays below 40 degrees. Do NOT rely on odor or appearance.

After you've eaten the foods from the refrigerator, eat perishables from the freezer. Foods from the freezer should only be eaten if they still have ice crystals in their interior or if the temperature in the freezer has not gone above 40 degrees.

Immediately throw away any food that may have come into contact with flood or storm water, and any food in containers with screw caps, crimped or twisted caps, snap lids, and snap open tops if they have been in contact with flood water.

Any of the following foods should be eaten before they sit unrefrigerated for more than two hours. Otherwise, toss them out:

- Raw meat, poultry, seafood
- Casseroles, stews soups
- Milk, cream, yogurt, soft cheese
- Cooked pasta, pasta salads
- Fresh eggs, egg substitutes

- Mayonnaise and tartar sauce
- Cream-filled pastries

These foods are OK for several days at room temperature:

- Fresh fruits and veggies
- Butter & margarine
- Opened jars of salad dressing, peanut butter, jelly, relish, mustard, ketchup, olives, pickles
- Hard and processed cheeses
- Fruit juices
- Fruit pies, bread, rolls, cakes, muffins

Shelf life of common food items:

- The following items should be eaten within six months: boxed powdered milk, dried fruit, dry crisp crackers, potatoes
- These items should be eaten within a year: canned meat and veggie soups, canned fruits and veggies, peanut butter and jelly, hard candy, canned nuts, vitamins
- The following items keep indefinitely as long as they are packaged properly and stored in the right conditions: wheat, soybeans, white rice, dry pasta, bouillon, vegetable oils, baking powder, salt, instant coffee, cocoa, tea, powdered milk, and powdered soft drinks.

2. Food for Disaster Kits & Food Storage

In a crisis you'll need to maintain your strength, and that requires eating nutritiously. Don't fill your kit with junk food. Here are some standard tips:

Emergency cooking: A cast iron two-burner propane stove, a propane camp heater/stove combo, a backpackers stove. There are many options.

- Plan the meals so you know what and how much to stock.
- Include a good variety of foods.
- Eat at least one well-balanced meal per day.
- Consume enough liquid (two quarts per day) to avoid dehydration.
- Consume the calories you'll need.
- Take vitamin, mineral, and protein supplements if necessary to ensure good nutrition.
- When choosing foods, consider how you will prepare them. They should require little or no cooking or water for preparation.
- If any of your food has to be heated, don't forget to put a stove and plenty of fuel in your disaster kit. Also,

make sure you have the can openers and knives or scissors you'll need to get into the food containers.

- Compact and lightweight foods are easier to manage and move around.
- Make a list of dates of when the food items need to be rotated (used and replaced).

A typical 72-hour kit should contain a selection of the following foods:

- Ready to eat canned meats, fruits, and vegetables
- Canned juices, milk, soup
- Sugar, salt, pepper
- High-energy foods—peanut butter, jelly, crackers, granola bars, trail mix
- Foods for anyone with special needs—infants, elderly, or those requiring special diets
- Dry pet food
- Comfort and stress foods like cookies, hard candy, sweetened cereals, suckers
- Instant coffee, hot chocolate, and tea bags
- Vitamin supplements
- One gallon of clean water per person or pet per day
- disposable plates, cups, utensils for nine meals per person

This could all be taken care of simply by tossing nine MREs per person into your storage. If you do, you're going to need a very big bag. MREs, or Meals Ready to Eat, require little or no preparation.

In the last couple of years the markets have been flooded with a huge menu of sports drinks or rehydration drinks with minerals for electrolyte replacement, and energy or power drinks whose main active ingredients are caffeine and taurine. Power drinks are designed to give a burst of energy. It makes sense to keep a couple of cans or bottles of both of these types of drinks on hand, to be used only when the situation merits it. Both of these types of drinks also come in powders.

If you're making a kit or planning food storage *for a couple of weeks or more*, you need to approach the task a little differently. Pay closer attention to long-term nutritional needs rather than focusing on short-term survival, energy, and hydration. Part of that supply is the normal food you

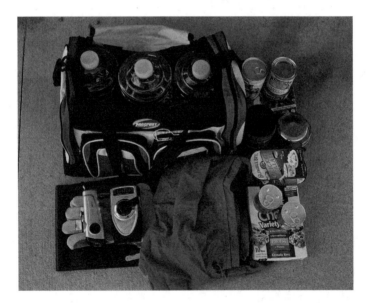

A simple 72-hour kit for one person. The food requires no stove or rehydration.

keep on your shelves. One strategy is to just increase how much of it you put on your shelves and rotate through it in your normal fashion. Another is to set aside a separate area for disaster food and water storage. However you decide to do it, here again are the standard pointers. Go heavy on food that's ready to eat or simple to prepare. In addition to the items listed above try:

- Shelf-stable boxes of juice and milk
- Crackers
- Jerky
- Instant oatmeal
- Dry milk
- Powdered drink mixes
- Instant pudding
- Dried soups
- Bouillon cubes or powder
- Instant rice or potatoes

If you're stocking up for the worst-case scenario, consider storing bulk staples and a variety of canned goods. Wheat, corn, beans, and salt can be purchased in bulk inexpensively and have a long shelf life. They're best purchased in nitrogen-packed cans. An adult could survive for a year with the following:

- Wheat, 250 pounds
- Powdered milk, 75 pounds
- Corn, 250 pounds
- Iodized salt, five pounds
- Beans, 125 pounds
- Fats and oils, 20 pounds or three gallons

- Vitamin C, 200 grams

This diet could get pretty boring after a few weeks, so plan to supplement your bulk foods with a selection of the items in the previous lists. Also, you'll need some way to grind the flour and corn.

Here's an alternative, more palatable list for an adult for one year:

- Flour, white enriched, 20 pounds
- Cornmeal, 40 pounds
- Beans, 30 pounds
- Pasta, 40 pounds
- Peas, split, one pound
- Lentils, one pound
- Dry soup mix, five pounds
- Peanut butter, four pounds
- Dry yeast, one pound
- Baking soda, one pound
- Baking powder, one pound
- Vinegar, one gallon

Again, plan on adding a few items from the yummier lists, but do not buy giant cans of foods that will need refrigeration after they're opened.

Before we end this chapter, let's answer your questions about food dates and storage methods.

Storing Dried Foods

Keep dry foods in airtight, moisture-proof containers away from direct light and in a cool location. Store-bought packages of staples should be stored in their original packages in airtight plastic containers so you'll have the containers for storing the leftovers when the package is opened. Stock a supply of ziplock food storage and freezer bags to store leftovers from opened containers of dry foods.

Food Dates

Sell by, expiration, and use by dates tell the store how long to display the item for sale. With proper refrigeration (including during transportation) meats will last a day or two beyond that date, other products as much as four days. If you buy eggs before the expiration date and you refrigerate them properly, they should be good for three weeks after the date you purchase them.

Best if used by and best if used before is the date to use the product at its best quality of flavor. It's NOT a final safety date or a final sale date.

Use by is the last date you should use or eat the product. Toss it out after that date.

Opened Canned Foods

Food not eaten should be removed from the can and stored in a nonmetallic container in the refrigerator or freezer. Food bottled in glass jars can be stored in the jars. Use the food within three to four days. If the food contains meat or fish of any kind, use it within two days or toss it out.

Chapter 8
Shelter and Evacuation

Your shelter is wherever you decide to hunker down and wait out the emergency. It may consist of sheltering "in place," at your home or at work, or even in your car. Or you might evacuate and find outside shelter at the home of a friend or relative, or at a motel or a community mass care facility.

The decision to stay or go might be made for you by the local authorities. When a disaster is imminent or has just happened, listen to the TV and radio and check the Internet to find out if instructions are being given. It may take some time for local authorities to make their initial assessments and decide what they want the public to do, and it will take more time to get that on the air or online. If you are aware of a large-scale emergency that has the potential to affect you, and you're unable to find out what's happening or what to do, your decisions might be based on your gut instincts. In any case, you'll be making your decisions based on the perception of the hazard, then choosing on-site sheltering or evacuation and off-site sheltering. The safest places will vary by hazard.

Wherever you decide to shelter, stay there until local authorities say it's safe to leave. Manage food and water as indicated in chapters 6 and 7. Assign shifts for 24-hour radio and safety watch so no important information or safety issues go unnoticed. Have at hand or take with you your disaster supplies kit.

1. Mass Care Shelters

Make no mistake about it, crowded mass care facilities can be unpleasant, but it beats the alternatives. Mass care shelters will probably have water, food, first aid supplies, medicine, first aid and medical providers, heating and air-cooling, basic sanitary facilities, blankets and cots.

If you go to a mass care facility, take your disaster kit with you to ensure you have what you need for yourself and for bartering. Do NOT take alcohol or firearms to the shelter unless you are told specifically by the shelter manager and the local authorities to do so. Also be aware that smoking will probably not be allowed inside the shelter.

2. Sheltering in Place

Sheltering in place means moving into a small interior room with few or no windows. This type of sheltering is likely to be used when hazardous materials, including chemical, biological, or radiological contaminants, are released into the environment. It could also be the result of weather emergencies, civil unrest, and many other causes. The recommendation to shelter in place will probably be given over radio, TV, Internet and possibly loudspeaker or telephone by local authorities. It may also happen that local authorities cannot respond and make those decisions before it's necessary for you to make a sheltering decision. In that case, if there's a large amount of debris in the air or the probability that the air is badly contaminated, your decision will probably be to shelter in place.

Here's a rather standard list of steps to take when sheltering in place at home:

Before the Event

- Bolt the walls of the structure securely to the foundation.
- Attach wall studs to roof rafters with metal hurricane clips
- Secure large appliances (especially the water heater) with flexible cable or metal stripping.

During the Event

- Close and lock all windows and exterior doors. Locking pulls the door tighter for a better seal.
- If there's a possibility of explosions, close window shades, blinds, and curtains.
- Turn off all fans, air conditioning, and heating systems.
- Close fireplace and stove dampers.
- Choose an interior room without windows or with as few windows as possible. In many homes this will be an interior bathroom. The room should be above ground level where heavier-than-air vapors and gases won't collect. Basements are not recommended for sheltering in place during hazardous materials emergencies because chemicals can seep in even if the windows are closed.
- Get your disaster supplies kit. Make sure the radio and lights work, and move the kit into the room.
- Move into the room. Bring the pets, too, and make sure there's enough food and water for them.
- If necessary, use the battery-operated LED or fluorescent lights in your disaster kit to light the room. One LED bulb will burn for days on a single battery. Do not burn anything for heat or light because of

the limited oxygen in your shelter space and the possibility of toxic combustion products (smoke, carbon monoxide). No candles.

- A POTS (Plain Old Telephone System) line to the room is preferable, but most of us don't wire our bathrooms for telephone service. If you have a cell phone, make sure you take it with you. Call your emergency contact and let them know where you are and what phone you'll be using. Keep the cell phone turned off to keep the battery charged.

- Use duct tape and plastic sheeting to seal the cracks around the door and any vents into the room.

- Establish a 24-hour radio or television and safety watch.

- Stay there until local authorities call for an evacuation or tell you to seek medical help.

Studies indicate that this type of shelter has adequate air for as much as three hours. Staying in the room too long can lead to suffocation. Individuals with respiratory problems will have less tolerance. Increased number of occupants, increased carbon dioxide emission rates, or increased activity resulting in oxygen depletion can decrease the length of time the shelter can be inhabited. The best protection occurs when the occupants enter the shelter before exposure and leave after exposure. Contaminated occupants might bring the contamination in with them and virtually nullify the protection. Contaminated occupants should do a quick "dry-decontamination" (strip down) before they enter the shelter. It you've done your disaster supplies kit right, there should be a set of clothes waiting in the shelter for you.

If there's a heavy chemical exposure, after two or three hours the shelter is likely to be compromised by contaminants leaking slowly into the room. Authorities by that time will probably recommend evacuation. Keep listening to the radio and follow their instructions completely.

When the emergency is over, ventilate the shelter to remove the contaminated air.

What Is a Safe Room?

A safe room is the modern version of what we used to call a *storm cellar*. Safe rooms are made using wood and steel or reinforced concrete, welded steel, or other strong materials. Safe rooms are usually built in a basement, on a slab-grade foundation, garage floor, or in an interior room on the lowest floor. The room is anchored securely to resist overturning. When building a safe room make sure the walls, ceilings, doors, and all connections are built to withstand extremely high winds and windborne debris. If the room is built below ground level, it must be flood-proof. FEMA has detailed plans for safe rooms on their Web site (www.fema.gov).

Shelter in Place at Work

Your business or workplace should use a means of alerting employees to shelter in place that is distinct from the alert to evacuate. Employees should be trained in SIP (shelter in place) procedures and their roles during an emergency.

When the decision to shelter in place has been made, here are some additional steps:

- Close the business.
- Ask customers to stay.

- Tell employees and customers to call their emergency contacts to tell them where they are and that they are safe.
- Turn on call forwarding or alternative answering systems. Change the recorded message to say that the business is closed and the staff and clients are sheltering there until authorities advise them to leave.
- Write down the names of everyone in the room.

Shelter in Place in Schools

In addition to the basic steps given above:

- Bring students and staff indoors. Ask visitors to stay.
- Close the school and activate the school's emergency plan.
- A phone with the school's listed number should be available in the shelter room, and a person should be assigned to answer calls.
- If multiple rooms are used, there should be a way to communicate between rooms (intercom, radio, etc.). Make announcements through the public address system.
- Change the voice-mail recording to say the school is closed and the kids are safe.
- Write the names of everyone in the shelter and call the school's emergency contact or local authorities to report who is there.

If you're a school administrator and your school doesn't already have some sort of plan in place, consider yourself negligent and get busy.

Community Containment vs. Shelter in Place

Community containment is a group of measures taken to control potential exposure to patients with contagious diseases. These steps include *isolation* and *quarantine*. Local, state, and federal health authorities are all empowered with the authority to order and enforce these measures. These agencies have what are referred to as "police powers" to "detain, medically examine, quarantine persons suspected of carrying communicable diseases" (42 CFR Parts 70 and 71). Isolation and quarantine may be voluntary or enforced. When enforced, failure to comply can result in arrest and criminal prosecution.

Isolation is the separation of persons known to have an illness from those who are healthy. The separation may be for focused delivery of health care (TB, for example).

Quarantine is separation or restriction of movement of persons or things that may have been exposed but may or may not become ill. Quarantine can apply to people, vehicles, buildings, cargo, animals, or anything else thought to be exposed. Isolation and quarantine are public health's best weapon against mass infection.

If you are placed on isolation or quarantine at home, take the following steps to protect your family and others:

- Stay at home, and when at home stay at least three feet away from other people. If possible, stay in a separate room with the door closed.
- Do not have visitors. Arrange to have deliveries placed outside your door, then you can bring them into the house.

- Cover your mouth and nose with a clean tissue when coughing or sneezing. Consider wearing a surgical mask.
- Everyone in the home should wash their hands frequently. Have some waterless hand sanitizer handy.
- Wash hard surfaces and anything handled by the isolated patient with a 1:10 solution of bleach and water (1½ cup of bleach to a gallon of water).
- Do not share dirty eating or drinking utensils.
- Wash clothes in hot or warm water and detergent.
- Household members living with an isolated patient should consider themselves on quarantine unless directed otherwise by the enforcing health department.

3. Evacuation

If authorities have issued an evacuation order or recommendation, do so immediately. Take minutes, not hours. During an evacuation you will be responsible for your own food, water, fuel, and supplies. This won't be a problem if you have a disaster supplies kit.

To prepare for Evacuation

- Know the evacuation plans for your building and community.
- Maintain a disaster supplies kit. Include copies of all your important documents, IDs, and some cash.
- Discuss possible evacuation procedures with your family and coworkers so they all know what to do.
- Choose, in advance, a destination outside the area and keep a road map and directions.

- Locate public emergency shelters in your area.
- Establish a check-in contact outside the area, whom all family members can report their status to. Make sure they all have the number.
- If an evacuation seems likely, keep a full tank of gas in the car. There will be no gas available during the evacuation.
- If you don't have a car, arrange for transportation with friends or neighbors, or contact the emergency management office and find out what plans are in place for buses or air evacuation.
- Don't forget about making plans for your pets.
- Know how to shut off the utilities, and have the tools to do it.

If Evacuation Is Imminent and You Know There's Time

- Let others know your destination. Leave a note or make some calls.
- Close and lock your doors and windows.
- Unplug appliances and electronics.
- Shut off water, gas, and electricity. If flooding is not likely and the gas is shut off, consider leaving the power on and the refrigerator plugged in.

If Evacuation Has Been Ordered

- Grab your disaster supplies kit. Remember your medications. Take along a bedroll for everyone: blankets or sleeping bags and ground insulation. Wear sturdy long-sleeved clothing and shoes if possible.

- Follow the recommended routes. Others may be blocked.
- Keep away from downed power lines.
- In flood conditions, be careful crossing bridges and stay out of washed-out roads.

When Returning Home

- Listen to the media for instructions. Return only when authorities say it's safe. Don't re-enter homes or buildings until authorities say it's safe.
- Be very cautious in buildings that have possible structural damage. Wear sturdy shoes or boots, heavy gloves, and safety goggles if available, to do your initial assessment of the building or when sifting through any debris.
- If you smell gas, leave immediately and tell the gas company or fire department. Don't switch on lights.
- Use flame- and spark-free lights when possible to avoid fires until the area is known to be safe from gas and flammables.
- If appliances are wet, switch off the power main and unplug the appliances. Give them plenty of time to dry out before you try to use them again.
- Inform your contacts that you and your family are safe.
- Watch for critters: bugs, snakes, spiders.
- Don't drink the local water until it's declared safe.

Chapter 9
First Aid and Light Rescue

In most disaster situations you will have little to work with. You'll be limited to what you already know and what supplies you have stockpiled. Fortunately, you will also have your common sense and your hands, which are the primary tools of first aid.

This book is not a substitute for formal first aid or medical training. We barely breeze through the very basics. Take a first aid course that includes CPR training. CPR training is necessary to learn how do deal with obstructed airways and to perform rescue breathing and cardiopulmonary resuscitation. An excellent free tutorial on CPR can be found at http://depts.washington.edu/learncpr/. The extra knowledge gained by taking a First Responder or Emergency Medical Technician course can make a big difference in your comfort zone while providing emergency care.

In a disaster we will be concerned with injuries and illnesses that threaten life and limb. Minor bumps and scrapes, tension headaches, bug bites, and the heartbreak of psoriasis will just have to wait.

In any situation, if there are life-or-limb-threatening injuries, call 911 or your local emergency services number immediately. In a major disaster the lines are likely to be tied up, and emergency crews will already be occupied. You may have to provide care for an extended period of time before more advanced medical care or transportation to the hospital is available.

1. Trauma

The initial patients in most disasters are likely to be trauma and burn patients, and that's where we'll start. Here are the steps you'll want to take when you have one or two patients who have suffered a significant mechanism of injury:

Assess and Manage Hazards

Don't play hero. A dead hero doesn't help anyone. Ensure your own safety first and your victim's safety from hazards (falling debris, rising water, severe temperatures).

Primary Survey

The primary survey is a search for life-threatening conditions. They are corrected as they are found. Always check in this order: Airway, Breathing, Circulation (A-B-C). Start by asking the patient if he or she is all right. If the answer is something like "Hell no, that damned wall just fell on me" then it's a good guess that the airway and breathing are OK for now.

A. Airway

- **Check for air movement.** If the patient is not talking then look, listen, and feel for air movement.
- **Open the airway** if no air movement is present. Use a head tilt, chin lift or a jaw thrust. You need to maintain the patient's neck in neutral position if you suspect a possible neck injury. (see photo).
- **Care of the airway** is important after the primary survey as well. Use the coma/recovery position

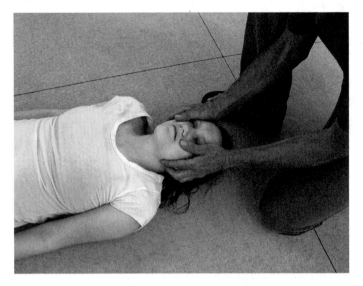

Jaw thrust and accompanying neck stabilization.

Coma position protects the airway of an unconscious
patient from aspiration.

(see photo) to protect the airway of an unconscious patient from the aspiration of vomit or secretions.

B. Breathing

- **Give artificial respiration** if needed. Take a CPR course beforehand. Use a CPR shield, or for mouth-to-mouth, pinch off the nose and make a seal over the patient's mouth. Breaths are given in pairs and should take one second each to make the chest rise. The normal adult breathing rate is 12 to 20 per minute.

- **Plug sucking chest wounds**. A sucking chest wound is a perforation in the chest that allows air to suck into the chest cavity. The air can eventually build up and collapse the lung. It should be plugged with whatever is handy. A tension pneumothorax is a complete collapse of the lung. It occurs when air enters, but does not leave, the space around the lung (pleural space). It is a life-threatening emergency that requires immediate treatment. If a sucking chest wound develops a tension pneumothorax, unplug it, then plug it again.

- **Splint a major flail chest**. A flail chest occurs when a segment of the thoracic wall breaks under extreme stress and becomes detached from the rest of the chest wall. It is a serious chest injury often associated with underlying pulmonary injury. Splinting it with a pillow or other splint decreases the work of breathing and decreases bleeding and pain.

C. Circulation

- **Check pulse. If no pulse, or if patient is unresponsive and not breathing, provide cardiac resuscitation**. Compressions for adult patients are given by compressing the center of the chest at the nipple line one and a half to two inches with the heel of the hand, at a rate of 100 per minute. The compressions to breaths ratio is 30:2.

- **Control severe bleeding** using direct pressure (pushing directly on the wound) and elevating the extremity. Dirty wounds can be treated later with antibiotics. Using pressure points is not often useful. Tourniquets are a desperate last resort that will result in the loss of the limb. If a tourniquet is used, it should be wide, tight, and should be removed only on orders from a doctor.

- **Assess and treat for shock**. Shock occurs when the body functions are threatened by not getting enough blood or when the major organs and tissues don't receive enough oxygen. Check the pulse. Patient going into shock will have a thready, rapid pulse and will be anxious, weak, or confused, and probably pale and thirsty. To treat for shock, **elevate the legs about 10 inches, reassure, and keep the patient** warm. Do not give foods or drinks.

To do a thorough check for injuries you're going to have to expose the patient—cut their clothes open. If you decide to do that, be sure to cover them again with something to prevent hypothermia.

Manage the Situation

Once the immediately life-threatening problems are controlled, pause and think of what needs to be done. Assign tasks and get everyone to work helping in some way.

Perform a focused **head-to-toe exam** looking for bruising, bleeding, deformity, tenderness, asymmetry and other unusual findings.

A. Head and Neurological Exam

Note that the big problem with head injuries is pressure building up inside the skull from bleeding and bruising. The pressure squeezes the brain and causes body functions to malfunction. When this happens:

- The level of consciousness goes down and the patient responds less to commands or pain.
- The nerve to an eye might be squeezed, causing one pupil to respond less to light or to dilate.
- Parts of the face or body might become weak, numb, or paralyzed, or seizures might occur.

A decreasing level of consciousness with pupil changes and paralysis or seizures indicates life-threatening pressure in the skull. The patient needs immediate evacuation to a hospital.

B. Neck and Spine

Check sensation and movement in each extremity. If the patient is unconscious, check the response to and movement from pain. Then **feel the entire spine for deformity and tenderness.** To know what a deformed spine is like, you need to know what a normal spine is like. Practice this exam beforehand. **If the spine is normal and sensation and movement are normal, but the victim sustained a severe mechanism of injury to the head or if for any other reason you suspect a neck trauma, treat it so.** Do not

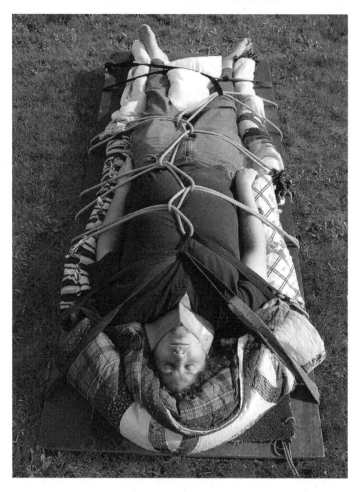

Total immobilization of the spine using a SAM splint and a door. Note how the patient is well padded to take up space and prevent movement of the head, neck, torso, and legs.

move or transport the patient without good immobilization of the spine. A stable patient with a suspected spine injury should not be moved until a proper backboard is available unless the patient has other problems that need urgent care (like life-threatening ABC problems). Stabilize the neck by applying an improvised C-collar (see photo) using a SAM splint or blanket/clothing rolls.

C. Chest

We've already discussed flail chest, tension pneumothorax, and sucking chest wounds. Ribs do not need to be splinted unless there's a flail chest. Collarbones can be splinted by splinting the arm to the body.

D. Abdomen and Pelvis

Remove or check underneath the patient's clothing. Imagine drawing a large cross intersecting through the injured person's belly dividing the abdomen into four sections, labeled from the patient's perspective: upper left, lower left, upper right and lower right. Feel each of the four sections of the abdomen with the palm of your hand, rolling your hand lightly from the base of the fingers to the wrist. Look for wounds, bruising, and distention and feel for any tenderness, swelling, rigid masses, and guarding (involuntary rigidity of the muscles). Listen for bowel sounds (it's a bad sign if they're absent).

Internal abdominal bleeding alone may cause shock. You can't control the bleeding, but you can treat for shock.

Press down on both hip bones and then inward toward each other. Press down on the pubic bone. Pain, grinding, or abnormal motion may indicate a fracture and possible internal bleeding, which can be severe.

E. Extremities

The entire exam should be completed before attempting to splint limbs. Treat dislocations as fractures. Irrigate and dress open fractures (bone ends that have punctured the skin). Here are the principles of splinting:

1. Long bone fractures: immobilize the joint above and joint below.
2. Fractures and dislocations around a joint: immobilize the bone above and the bone below.
3. Check pulse/capillary refill (see photo 9-5) AND movement/sensation BEFORE and AFTER splinting.
4. In general, splint it as it lies; under axial traction, a long bone may be gently straightened, if there's no great amount of pain or resistance.
5. Thigh fractures (aka femur fractures) should be splinted with a traction splint, if other injuries allow and somebody who is trained is there to apply it.
6. Keep checking circulation to make sure the swelling hasn't made the splint too tight.

F. The Backside

Don't forget the backside. Log roll the patient as a unit if you suspect a spine injury. Check the back for wounds, bruises, and deformity.

Basic First Aid for Other Common Injuries

Burns and frostbite are both local tissue injuries caused by extremes temperature. They are classified similarly based on the depth and severity of tissue damage and are treated similarly. Deep tissue injuries will appear white, gray, or black. Treatment for burns includes removing the source of heat from the burn, cooling the burn, and covering it. Do no use ice or apply antiseptics or ointments, and do not remove shreds of tissue or break blisters. For extensive or third degree burns, always treat for shock. Treatment for frostbite includes removing the source of cold from the frostbite, warming the frostbite (with an underarm or tepid tap water), and covering it. Heat and cold injuries can both cause dehydration and become infected. Get medical help for deep tissue injuries.

Wound care includes controlling bleeding, cleaning, and bandaging. Clean the wound with soap and water. Then apply a dressing on the wound and secure with a bandage. If there's no active bleeding, change the dressings and check the wound every four to six hours. If there is active bleeding, place a new dressing over the old dressings and continue applying direct pressure and elevation. Do not attempt to close a wound unless you're trained to do so.

Sprains and fractures have many of the same symptoms. It may be impossible to correctly diagnose the injury without an X-ray. Sprains should be treated as fractures. Splints can be made from soft or rigid materials. They can also be made by binding two adjacent body parts together in several places ("buddy splint"). Use the RICE concept to treat other joint and soft tissue injuries: Rest, Ice, Compression (with an elastic bandage), and Elevation. Take OTC (over-the-counter) pain meds for pain.

2.   The Brutal Reality

Author's note: While I certainly recommend the reader take a CPR course, I think it's only fair to make two unpleasant truths perfectly clear. First, CPR is only occasionally successful, and the outlook is very poor for patients whose heart and lungs are stopped due to trauma or severe bleeding.

The second truth is that in a multiple-casualty situation where there are dying and injured patients all around, the goal of whoever is still standing should be to provide the greatest benefit to the greatest number of people. This means you need to recognize those who are in need of treatment and those who can wait. This is called triage, or casualty sorting, and it's just one of those unfortunate aspects of disasters. It's what the responders to your incident will do, and it's what you should do. It's important to not become involved in treating the first couple of patients you see. You need to reach each patient as soon as possible, conduct a quick assessment, and assign them to a category. You only stop to quickly correct airway and severe bleeding problems. Others who arrive as you're doing this can provide follow-up treatment. The bottom line is that someone in pulmonary or cardiac arrest just simply will not be resuscitated, even if it's possible to do so. The reason is simple: successful resuscitation of the dead is not likely and attempting it wastes precious time and resources that could be used to help the living.

If you're a layperson with limited first aid training, you'll just have to triage using common sense. Professional and paraprofessional responders train with the START system. The START (Simple Triage And Rapid Treatment) system lets responders triage each patient in 60 seconds or less, based on three observations: breathing, circulation, and mental status. START begins with a loud verbal command to "get up and walk over here!" Those that do are green-tagged (priority 3) and are referred to as the "walking wounded." Black-tagged or priority 4 patients are considered dead or unsalvageable based on their lack of breathing after a single attempt to establish their airway. Red tagged or priority 1 patients are "immediate" patients who are given the highest treatment priority based on their resolved respiratory arrest, a respiratory rate of over 30 per minute, a capillary refill of greater than two seconds, or their failure to follow simple commands. Everyone else is tagged yellow (priority 2). The patients are treated and transported according to those priorities.

3.   The First Aid Kit

The best first aid kit is the one you know how to use. Putting in a lot of fancy medical gadgets that you can't use makes no sense. The following is a typical kit for the family or office, based on the average person's level of first aid training.

- First aid manual (anything will do, but the pocket-sized wilderness first aid manuals are more appropriate for disaster situations).
- LED headlamp & batteries.
- Surgical masks.
- Sterile adhesive bandages ("Band-Aids").
- Latex gloves (several pair). Note that in a multiple-casualty incident the flimsy latex exam gloves that

are typically carried in first aid kits will be ripped to shreds. Dishwashing gloves will last much longer and can be sanitized in a bucket of 1:10 bleach and water in between patients.

- 2-inch sterile gauze pads (12).
- 4-inch sterile gauze pads (12).
- Triangular bandages (3–6).
- 2-inch sterile roller bandages (3–6).
- 3-inch sterile roller bandages (3–6).
- 1-inch hypoallergenic cloth adhesive tape ("first aid" tape) (2 rolls), or duct tape.
- Scissors—EMT trauma-shears will cut through the toughest material and will outlast bandage scissors.
- Tweezers or forceps (2).
- Needles (various sizes).
- Chemical cold packs (3–6).
- Pocket CPR mask (get the full-mask variety, like the Laerdal pocket mask, that is compatible with bag-valve breathing devices that responders will bring with them).
- Tongue depressors (12).
- Antibacterial soap (1 bottle).
- Alcohol wipes (12).
- Provodine-iodine wipes (12).
- Antibiotic ointment (1 tube).
- Hydrogen peroxide (1 bottle).
- Thermometer (digital).
- Assorted safety pins (diaper pins are stronger and last longer).
- Petroleum jelly (1 tube).
- Hand sanitizer (1–2 bottles).

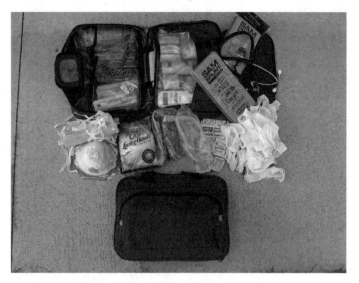

Example of a family-sized first aid kit.

- Sunscreen (1 tube).
- DEET bug repellent (2 tubes, cans, or many individual wipes).
- OTC pain reliever (aspirin, acetaminophen, ibuprofen, etc.) (1 bottle).
- OTC antidiarrheal medication (1 bottle or box).
- Antacid (1 bottle).
- Laxative (1 box).
- Vitamins (1 bottle).
- Infant medications.
- Syrup of Ipecac (1 bottle).
- Activated charcoal (1 bottle).
- Prescription medications as needed.
- Paper and pencil.

Consider stocking your kit with acetaminophen and codeine ("Tylenol 3"). It's an excellent pain reliever, antidiarrheal, and cough suppressant.

4.   Doing Vital Signs & History

The last item, paper and pencil, is for documentation. Vital signs and history are the eyes that responders and medical providers use to initially diagnose and treat their patients. Vital signs trends are a tip-off to the current status and prognosis of the patient. Any seriously injured or ill patient in your care should have vitals taken and recorded at least every 15 minutes, and preferably more. The key vital signs are easy to take, even without medical equipment:

Level of Consciousness: One of the first things that happens in many deteriorating conditions (shock, hypothermia, heat stroke, and high fever) is a drop in the level of consciousness. The patient "gets stupid." Note if the patient is conscious and alert, disoriented or not alert, or unconscious. To be even more specific, note if the patient is alert, not alert but responds to loud verbal stimulus, responds only to painful stimuli, or is totally unresponsive. The normal state is conscious, oriented, and alert.

Pulse: Pulse is easily taken by placing the fingers on the notch of the wrist on the thumb side of the hand. This is the radial pulse. Count the pulse for 30 seconds and multiply by 2 (or for 15 seconds and multiply by 4). If you can't find a radial pulse, try the brachial pulse midway up along the inside of the upper arm. For an unconscious person without a brachial pulse, try the carotid pulse in the groove of the neck, just off the voice box. If all else fails, put your ear to the chest and listen for a heartbeat. The different qualities of a pulse have different meanings. Rate relates to oxygenation. Strength relates to blood pressure. Regularity relates to cardiac function. You can tell a lot from a pulse, but it takes some study and practice. The normal adult pulse is 60–100 per minute, strong and regular.

Skin color: Various skin colors and qualities tell specific stories. Red face, blue face, yellow face. Wet face, dry face, hot face, cold face. It all indicates something specific. Watch it and write it down. The normal skin condition is pink, dry, and warm to touch.

Blood pressure is a useful vital sign but very difficult to accurately measure without special equipment (stethoscope and blood pressure cuff). A ballpark estimate of systolic pressure can be derived from taking the pulse. If a radial pulse is present, the systolic is at least 80; 70 for the brachial pulse; and 60 for the carotid. The normal systolic pressure for an adult is 80 plus the age (+10 for males).

Respiration: Again, the rate and quality of respirations can tell medical providers a lot. Rate is an indication of oxygenation, and depth and patterns can be indicators of acid-base problems, brain injuries, and respiratory diseases. Count the respirations in 30 seconds and multiply by two. Don't tell the patient you're counting. Normal respirations in an adult are 12–20 per minute.

The history should be obtained from the patient and bystanders during the focused assessment. This is summarized in the acronym SAMPLE.

It consists of information that could help determine the course of treatment for the patient, including the patient's name and age, Signs and symptoms, Allergies, current Medications, Prior medical history, time of Last meal, and the Events or mechanism of injury or illness.

5.   Medical Emergencies

Medical conditions can be aggravated by disasters and the environments they create. Infections will occur. Women will continue to have babies. Heart attacks will probably increase. These things require medical care—not first aid. Unfortunately it's possible that a disaster will cut you off from hospital- or clinic-based medical care. This is where community planning and advanced training and preparation pay off.

Those of you who may be concerned about the possibility of being stranded away from medical care may wish to consider purchasing one or more of several self-help medical manuals that have been written to provide remote villages and backcountry groups with basic medical and health information that will cover most problems. These books include:

1. *Special Operations Forces Medical Handbook* (not currently available).
2. *Austere Medicine*—a printable, online survival medical guide for "the end-times" at www.endtimesreport. com.
3. *Field Guide to Wilderness Medicine*, Paul S. Auerbach, Howard Donner, and Eric Weiss.
4. *Where There Is No Doctor*, David Werner—one of several excellent books available for download at http://www.hesperian.org. Hard copies are available for purchase.
5. *Medicine for Mountaineering and Other Wilderness Activities*, James A. Wilkerson.

These books are appropriate for users with specific levels of first aid or medical training. If you have limited training and want a book that will walk you through the important stuff, get a copy of *Where There Is No Doctor*.

Modified Patient Assessment

With medical patients (as opposed to trauma patients) you'll want to get a better history that includes some information about the onset and quality of the problem. Let the patient talk, and when he/she is finished, ask them if there's anything else they can tell you about it.

In addition to checking the ABCs, you're going to want to get the SAMPLE history and a set of vitals. Check the vitals frequently. While you're talking to the patient or witnesses, try to get PQRST information:

P — provocation and position (location of pain)

Q—quality of pain (sharp, dull, crushing)

R— radiation (does it travel to another part of the body?)

S—severity (on a scale of 1–10) and other symptoms

T—timing and triggers (occasional, constant, only when I eat, stand, etc.)

This information may not mean much to you medically, but if you have to take care of the patient for hours or days, it will help you decide how to treat his/her symptoms.

Allergic Reaction (Anaphylaxis)

Occurs after exposure to an allergen (food, insect sting, medicine) to which a person is already extremely sensitive. Allergic reactions can be life-threatening.

Signs and symptoms (S/S): Swelling and redness of the skin; itchy raised rash (like hives); swelling of the throat; wheezing and/or coughing; rapid irregular pulse; tightness in the chest; headache; vomiting; diarrhea; dizziness or unconsciousness

Treatment (Tx): ABCs; call for help. Take and record pulse and respiratory rate (RR). If carrying their own adrenaline (Epi-Pen), use it at once: assist the patient (pt) to give his/her own medication. If conscious, help pt to sit in the easiest breathing position. If unconscious, check ABCs and be ready for CPR.

Asthma Attack

A slow or sudden narrowing of the bronchial tubes, often triggered by allergies.

S/S: Wheezing, difficulty exhaling; coughing; gasping; anxiety, panic, cyanosis. If wheezing disappears and the pt becomes drowsy or confused, respiratory arrest is probably imminent.

Tx: Call for help. Make the pt comfortable, usually sitting upright and leaning forward. Ensure adequate fresh air. Tell pt to take slow deep breaths. Help with administration of meds, usually 2–4 puffs, one at a time with breath with each puff and 4 breaths in between. If no improvement, repeat meds. If attack is severe, continue with puffs at 4 every 4 minutes for kids, 6–8 every 4 minutes for adults. If the patient is conscious and alert, 3 cups of strong coffee (not decaffeinated) will help dilate the bronchial tubes. Caffeine is related to theophylline, the active ingredient of many inhalers.

Chest Pain or Discomfort

Angina is caused by a lack of oxygen to heart muscle. It's brought on by exertion and relieved by rest or nitroglycerin tablets. Any chest pain not resolved in 15 minutes needs prompt advanced medical care.

A heart attack is actual death of cardiac muscle that occurs when the blood supply to the heart is blocked or severely reduced.

Angina S/S: pain or discomfort in the middle of the chest; radiating to neck and arms; onset with exercise or emotional stress; pain relieved by rest or medication.

Heart attack S/S: similar to angina plus severe vice-like chest pain (CP), anxiety and confusion, shortness of breath (SOB), nausea and vomiting (N/V), irregular pulse, sensation of palpations or skipped beats, sometimes immediate collapse.

Tx: Stop any activity and have pt lie down and rest. Assist pt in taking prescribed angina meds. Nitroglycerine is taken under the tongue, not chewed or swallowed. one tablet every 5 minutes for 15 minutes (up to three tablets total). For heart attack, monitor ABCs and call for help. Give aspirin 300 mg (one tablet) with water. Don't give aspirin to those allergic, asthmatics, or those on anti-coagulants. Monitor vitals and prepare to give CPR. Give no food and only tiny sips of water.

Diabetic Emergency

With diabetes the patient has difficulty maintaining a normal glucose balance.

Hypoglycemia S/S: Onset is usually fast (minutes to hours). Pale, hungry, sweating, weak, confused, aggressive. This is often referred to as insulin shock because the patient has either taken too much insulin or has not eaten enough food to balance with the insulin they took.

Hyperglycemia S/S: Onset is usually slow (days to weeks). Thirsty, needs to pee, hot dry skin, smell of acetone breath.

Tx: ABCs. Call for help. If conscious and low sugar suspected: give sweet food or drink every 15 minutes until recovery. If conscious and high sugar suspected: allow pt to self-administer insulin. Give sugar-free fluids until recovery.

Check the patient's blood sugar level with their glucometer or a glucose stick. Normal blood glucose levels are 70–110. If a stick is unavailable and you're unsure which diabetic problem it is, treat for low sugar. The extra sugar will do no immediate harm.

Seizure

A seizure is a sudden involuntary muscle contraction commonly caused by uncontrolled electrical activity in the brain. The seizure can be local (focused in one part of the body) or generalized. Seizures can be caused by epilepsy, brain disorders and injuries including stroke, poisoning and overdose, heat stroke, fever, and imbalances of glucose or electrolytes.

S/S: Feeling hot, exhausted, weak. Persistent headache. Thirst and nausea. Pale, cool clammy or flushed skin. As the condition becomes more serious the pulse becomes rapid and weak. The body temperature becomes high ("heat stroke") and the patient can no longer sweat. Confusion may progress to seizures and unconsciousness.

Tx: ABCs. Protect the pt from injury. Do not restrict movement. Do not place anything in the mouth. Manage injuries: place on side as soon as possible. Do not disturb if pt falls asleep or seems catatonic or very confused (this may be a recovery period called a "post-ictal state"). Check vitals. Seek help if seizure longer than 5 minutes or another seizure quickly follows, or the pt has been injured. If fever is suspected cause, cool with cool wet cloths. Give no food, and only tiny sips of water when the patient is fully alert again.

Heat-Induced Conditions

S/S: Feeling hot, exhausted, weak. Persistent headache. Thirst and nausea. Giddiness and faintness, or irritability and confusion that may progress to seizure and unconsciousness. Pale cool clammy skin or flushed skin. Rapid weak pulse. Normal to high body temperature.

Tx: Heat exhaustion: Lie pt down in a cool place with circulating air. Loosen tight clothing and remove unnecessary clothing. Sponge with cold water. Give fluids to drink. Seek help if casualty vomits or does not recover promptly.

Heat Stroke: ABCs. Apply cold packs or ice to neck, groin, armpits. Cover with a wet sheet. Call for help. If fully conscious, give fluids.

Cold-Induced Conditions

Hypothermia S/S: Early: feeling cold, shivering, clumsiness and slurred speech, apathy and irrational behavior, possible slow heart rate. Severe: declining level of consciousness (LOC), shivering stops, pulse hard to find.

Tx: ABCs. Remove to warm, dry place. Protect from wind, rain, sleet, and cold wet ground. Maintain in horizontal position. Remove wet clothing. Warm casualty—place between blankets or in sleeping bag, and wrap in space blanket or similar. If severe, do NOT use direct radiant heat. Cover head to maintain body heat. Give warm drinks if conscious. No alcohol.

Poisoning

S/S: Abdominal pain, drowsiness, N/V, burning pains from mouth to stomach, difficulty breathing, tight chest, blurred vision, breath odor, change of skin color with blueness around lips, sudden collapse.

Tx: Do not attempt to induce vomiting. ABCs. Call for ambulance (and fire department if atmosphere contaminated with smoke or gas). If the pt is conscious: Check for danger. Listen to pt, try to determine type of poison and amount. Call poison control (fill in your local number here): _____

_____

Snake and Spider Bites

The beasties are going to be looking for shelter and high ground, too, and you might find some unusual visitors bunking with you during a disaster. Learn to recognize the venomous snakes and spiders in your region.

First Aid for Non-Poisonous Snake Bites

Remove all constrictive clothing, shoes, or jewelry from bitten hand or bitten leg. Wash the wound with soap and water. Place a cold pack or ice pack on the wound, 15 minutes on and 15 minutes off. Keep victim calm. Do not give sedatives or alcohol.

Poisonous Snakes

Be prepared beforehand by learning to recognize local venomous species. Stay calm. Watch ABCs. Do not waste time trying to capture or kill the snake. Do not apply an ice pack or cold pack to the wound. Keep the bite at the level of the heart. Consider applying a constrictive band (NOT a tourniquet) just above the bite between the bite and the heart. The band should be wide and snug, but loose enough to slip one finger underneath the band and still feel a pulse beyond it. Constricting bands may have some delaying effect with neurotoxins (e.g., cobras and coral snakes) but may increase local tissue damage with other types of toxins (rattlesnakes, vipers, etc.). Do not cut into the wound. Do not suck the wound with your mouth. Get medical help as soon as possible. Many bites are dry bites, and if no serious swelling occurs at the site of a viper (e.g., rattlesnake) bite within 30 minutes, the pt will probably have no problems. Clean and watch the site for infection.

Spider and Scorpion Bites

There are more than 50 spiders and several scorpions in the U.S. that have venom that can cause local reactions similar to a bee sting or mosquito bite. These are where those unexplained bites that you find in the morning come from. The bite will be mildly swollen for a couple of days. There may be some stinging and numbness with a scorpion sting. Scorpion stings, spider bites, and snake bites are rarely fatal in North America, but elsewhere they're a serious problem.

If it's a known black widow bite, apply an ice pack to the site for 20 minutes to slow the spread of the venom. Do not apply a tourniquet. Many bites are dry bites, but those that are serious will produce abdominal pain, chest tightness, and muscle cramps. Get medical help.

Recluse, hobo, and wolf spider bites may produce some necrosis and invite infection at the bite site. Clean and dress the site. Do not apply ice. Necrosis will start with a blister or a purple bite site. Redness at the site in the first 24 hours is due to venom. After that, redness and yellow drainage at the site indicates infection. Get medical help.

Insect Bites

Watch for signs of a severe allergic reaction. Remove a stinger if still present by scraping the back of a knife or other straight-edged object across the stinger. Wash the site with soap and water. Place ice (wrapped in a cloth) on the site of the sting for 10 minutes. Repeat 10 minutes later and as needed. If necessary, take an antihistamine or apply creams that reduce itching. Watch for signs of infection (such as increasing redness, swelling, or pain).

6. Extended Care in Remote or Stranded Settings

If there's a chance you're going to be waiting for help for more than a day, keep these tidbits in mind:

- Develop some long-term and back-up plans for first aid care and for getting the patient to the hospital.

- Pain management: a patient without activities to distract him/her is likely to focus on pain and may need some medication to control it.

- A patient needing surgery should have nothing to eat or drink for 8 hours before surgery.

- Patients with airway problems should have nothing to eat or drink. They need IV fluids.

- Very ill patients who will not need surgery or who do not have airway problems can take small sips of water several times per hour.

- Patients with minor problems can eat and drink what they want.

- Watch for signs of dehydration: dark urine, furrowed tongue, parched lips tenting, thirst. Severe dehydration can result in shock.

- Fecal impaction is common in immobilized patients and can be brought on by dehydration, low food intake, and narcotic pain medication. It's a common problem in shelter groups because of the reluctance to defecate in close proximity to other people. Severe impaction will require some digital help . . . and yes, that means your finger.

- If you have an unconscious patient or an immobilized patient, watch the airway closely. Turn them or suction them when they vomit. Effective suction is difficult to do with improvised suction equipment.

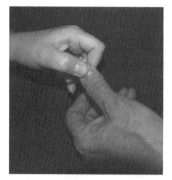

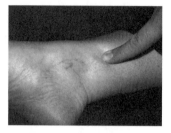

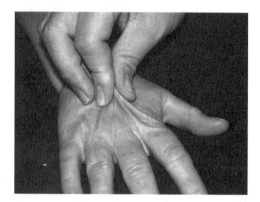

Reach out and touch someone. When you're doing extended care, a lot of information can be gleaned from the condition of the skin by pinching the nail bed of a finger or the skin over the sternum so it blanches. If the color doesn't return within three seconds, it may indicate low blood pressure (shock), bad circulation in the limb, or a cold extremity. Tenting is a condition in which pinched skin stays pinched when it's released. In a young healthy person it can indicate serious dehydration. Deep pitting can indicate edema, which can result from certain heart or kidney problems. To check for pitting, push a finger into swollen tissue. If it stays deeply depressed when it's released, it's pitting.

- Fluid can accumulate in the lungs of immobilized patients. Have the patient breath deeply and cough frequently. Patients who can walk should do so briefly every day.
- Patients who have been immobilized or bed-ridden for over 24 hours can develop bedsores. Change the patient's position every two hours and pad pressure points. Treat bedsores like other wounds.

7.   Light Rescue

Search and rescue operations are dangerous functions that should be reserved for trained, professional or paraprofessional rescuers. Unfortunately, like a lot of other things, it will initially be the decision of those left standing whether to jump in and risk their own lives. An interesting statistic should serve as a stark reminder about the risk: in the Mexico City earthquake, more rescuers (good Samaritans and professionals alike) were killed in the rescue efforts than were non-rescuers killed during the quake itself. In any scenario, the decision to do search and rescue should be based on the risks involved and the need to do the greatest good for the greatest number. The goals should be to be safe and to rescue as many as possible as soon as possible. That will be done by getting the lightly trapped victims out first. Learn to do this correctly by taking a CERT (community emergency response team) course. Contact your local Citizen's Corps office or the state emergency management office for information on CERT training.

If you're that lucky person left standing, part of your decision will be to determine whether evacuation is needed for survivor safety. You should assist with that before attempting search or rescue operations.

Take some time to size up the situation and get an idea of how many victims may be trapped, and where they are likely to be (e.g., where are the voids that might have been created, and where are likely areas where groups might have gathered.) The search should be accomplished using a systematic, thorough method that will not require it to be done over and which provides some minimal documentation. Here's the basic search methodology:

- Call out and listen carefully.
- Never enter a burning or unstable structure.
- Search multi-story buildings from the bottom up or the top down. Be consistent.
- The wall is your lifeline. Keep your right hand on the right wall or left hand on the left wall to stay oriented.
- Triangulate flashlights to give a single location better illumination.
- Search with a buddy. Do NOT go alone.
- Mark searched rooms or areas with an X on or near the door. CERT teams who enter the area will notice these markings. On top of the X write the time and date of the search. On the right side of the X write any hazard information. On the bottom of the X write how many victims are still inside. If the room or area is hazardous, draw a box around the X.
- Document the results of your searches on a piece of paper. Give it to the CERTS or other responders when they arrive.

Once the victims have been located and triaged, they can then be removed if safety concerns permit. A dead or injured hero only adds to the chaos, so recognize your limits and be safe.

The method of extrication will depend on the number and abilities of helpers you have at hand, the stability of the environment, and the condition of the patient.

Let the victim help him or herself as much as possible. Remove obstacles and debris and allow them to get themselves out. Those with head and spine injuries should be stabilized and immobilized as much as reasonably possible before moving them.

When lifting a patient or any heavy load, keep the back straight and keep the load close to your body. Push up with your legs and stand up with the load rather than bending over and pulling the load up with arm and back muscles.

Special Rescue Situations

Swift-water rescue, confined space rescue, complicated automobile extrication, and high angle situations require special skills and experience. Send for help and wait for the experts.

Some things you can do in water situations include reaching out to the swimmer with a pole or stick, throwing a rope or a flotation device, or paddling or rowing out on an improvised raft or boat. If you are isolated and need to swim out for help in deep but calm water, put empty plastic bottles in a backpack or bag and put it on or hold it in front of you like a swimming board. Do not enter moving water deeper than mid-calf or of unknown depth, and never tie into a rope in moving water. See the section on floods in chapter 10.

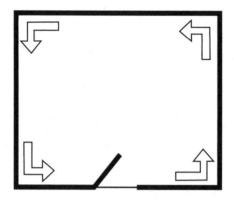

Systematic room search pattern. Typically it's done along the wall going counterclockwise, keeping the right hand in constant contact with the wall. Interior portions of the room can be probed one-handed with a pole, and light can be triangulated from several directions to provide the best visual coverage.

MRC members practicing patient extrication using a simple two-person leverage and cribbing operation. Leverage and cribbing can be used to remove debris and avoid more injuries. Wear whatever protective gear you have available. Crib with whatever solid material you can find.

Chapter 10
Specific Hazards

1. Drought

The Basics

Drought is a lack or deficiency of rainfall or snowpack over an extended period ranging from months to years or decades, resulting in a critical insufficiency in the water supply for a particular region. Drought is crushing for agriculture, and it has serious detrimental effects on industry, commerce, the economy, the environment, and social well-being. The effects of drought can include:

- Death of livestock
- Crop failure
- Famine and malnutrition, worsened by poverty
- Reduced water quality due to concentration of contaminants and pollutants
- Dehydration and disease
- Wildfires in dry vegetation
- Desertification
- Civil unrest, riots, and war
- Mass migration

The Jargon

Desertification—a process in which fertile land turns into desert.

Meteorological—pertaining to the science of weather
Hydrologic—pertaining to the study of water
Agricultural—pertaining to farming

Protecting Yourself and Your Family

Unfortunately, drought is one of those natural occurrences that's hard to be effective against. Community strategies might eventually include water restrictions and the use of alternative water sources, such as desalinization, recycling, drilling, and regulated planting of selective crops. Most of these strategies require the focus and cooperation of individuals, and that's very difficult to get. Americans have a difficult time letting go of their precious lawns and landscapes.

Unless you've had the foresight, space, and patience to store enormous quantities of water, there's little you can do about drought except being conscientious about your water use.

Adding some cash and goods to your disaster supply kit would probably be just as or more effective than trying to store and maintain huge tanks of emergency water. As drought progresses those who have the cash or goods to barter for water will get what they need. Those who don't won't.

2.   Data Loss

The Basics

Data loss itself is a disaster, and is likely to occur during any other major disaster. We have become almost totally reliant on computers for communication, information storage, and financial management. The loss of this capability and the data already committed to it can be devastating to individuals as well and major companies and government agencies, and it could be weeks or months—maybe never—before the data can be restored or recovered.

In a nutshell, there are four basic causes of data loss. The first is **corruption** due to viruses. The second is **mechanical failure** due to power surges or failures, water damage, and the like. The third is **theft**. The fourth is **operator error**.

Dealing with potential data loss is a matter of doing a risk assessment and formulating plans to deal with those risks. Your plans should enable you to resume business without serious disruption. Your insurance policies should cover hardware and software. Large businesses should consider hacker insurance.

The Jargon

CPU—Central Processing Unit. The brains of the computer. It handles all the operations.

Data—Any type of information. In a computer, data is stored in files.

Gigabyte—G; a measurement of memory equivalent to 1,024 megabytes.

Hacker—A person who has gained unauthorized access into a computer system.

Hard drive—A device that stores data and programs, usually connected permanently to the main computer housing.

Hardware—The physical equipment that makes up the computer system: monitor, keyboard, disk drives.

Modem—A device that transmits digital data from your computer across analog phone lines

Peripherals—Hardware that's added to the CPU, such as a printer, monitor, mouse, keyboard, or external drive.

Power surge—A sudden increase in power.

Server—A computer that delivers information and services to other computers linked by a network.

Software—Computer programs.

UPS—Uninterruptible power supply containing a battery that provides a continuous supply of power in case of a power failure and circuitry to protect electronic equipment from power surges.

Virus—A computer program designed to attach itself to a file and replicate and spread from file to file, destroying data or interrupting computer operations.

Protecting Yourself, Your Family, and Your Business

Here are six steps you can take to ensure a comfortable level of safety for your data system.

Protect Your System

If your data systems are critical to your financial well-being, get help from an expert who can assess the threats and minimize the risks to your data systems. He/she will probably insist that you:

- Grant system access on a very selective basis. Limit access as much as possible. At your office, limit physical access to only those employees who are required to use the computer to do their jobs.

- Allow business use only on business computers. There should be no personal software allowed.

- Take extreme caution when downloading anything.

- Not load any software that isn't shrink-wrapped and from a dealer you trust.
- Use passwords and change them frequently.
- Give your computers periodic checkups and run antiviral software daily.

Protect Your Hardware

Protect your hardware by taking the following precautions:

- Don't allow food or drinks at the computer.
- Have the CPU and the peripherals cleaned by a professional on a regular basis. Dust and dirt are trouble.
- Keep waterproof tarps or covers handy to protect equipment. Elevate equipment to keep it away from flood water and secure equipment to keep it from falling to the ground.
- Have an alternative power source.
- Use surge protectors or a UPS (uninterrupted power supply). This is especially important if your power is backed up by a generator. If the power fails and the generator kicks in, the generator may have trouble keeping the power stable during the surge. Replace surge protectors every year or so. If the generator isn't automatic, switch everything off before starting it up.
- When the air crackles (close lightning, electrical shorts, etc.), disconnect the modem.
- Maintain the temperature and humidity. Excessive warmth and dampness are more trouble.
- Keep hardware and software licenses up to date. Maintain hardcopy records in a secure location.

Protect Your Files

Backing up your files is the single most important step in mitigating a data-loss disaster:

- NEVER be in a position where re-entry of data will require more than a day's work.
- Use a removable data storage device and back up your on-site data on a regular basis, preferably at least daily. You can take it with you when you evacuate. A 250G external hard drive can be purchased for under $200, 160G for around $100. A 30G iPod costs under $200 and might be used as incentive for employees to back up their files. Consider having laptops or notebook computers for employees so they can take their data and computers off-site and continue working seamlessly.
- Back up your drive and all of your data at least weekly and keep a set stored off-site. Use a secure server more than 50 miles from the office, or use an online back-up service. Or place the backup in a fireproof safe, at a satellite office, at home, or at a commercial data center.
- Include in your backups all key business and family or personal information, including budgets, client lists, contact information, sales and tax records, insurance policies, and banking transactions.
- Keep a clear paper trail that will allow easy re-entry of data.

Protect your inventory

Pre-analyze your supply and demand, so you'll know what you'll need to keep working.

Backing up data: An external drive (160G), an USB
mass data storage device, an external flash drive (2G),
a notebook computer. CDs are of limited value.

Develop a Data Disaster
Attachment to Your Disaster Plan

In the attachment, answer the following questions:

- What concrete measures are in place and who is responsible for them?
- Even with the data backed up, how will we restore it and get it running again?
- If computers are not an option, how can paper-based systems be used and are they in place?

Stay up to Date

A year or so after the publishing date, this material will be outdated. Both the threats and solutions will be more complicated.

3.   Fire

The Basics

Fire requires three elements to exist: heat, fuel, and oxygen. This is often referred to as the fire triangle. When fire ignites, it needs all of these elements to accomplish the chain reaction required to maintain the fire. Remove any of the elements, and the fire goes out.

In many parts of the world fires are put into one of four classes:

Class A–Ordinary combustibles like wood, cloth, paper, plastics
Class B–Flammable liquids and gases
Class C–Electrical equipment
Class D–Combustible metals

The class of fire determines the method of fire suppression.

The Jargon

Arson—The crime of intentionally setting destructive fire
Combustible—Capable of igniting and burning
Conduction—The transfer of heat from one object to another when they're in contact
Convection—The transfer of heat by movement of a heated substance (e.g., heated air currents)

Crown fire—A fire that jumps along the tops of trees due to wind

Fire Triangle— Triangle defining the essential elements of fire: heat, fuel, and oxygen in a chain reaction

Flammable—Easily ignited and capable of burning quickly. Technically, the difference between flammable and combustible is defined by a material's flash point

Ground fire—Fire burning along the forest floor

Standpipe—A vertical pipe leading from a water supply, especially one that provides an emergency water resource

Structure fire—Fire in a building

Surface fire—Slow-moving fire at tree or brush level

Wildfire—An unplanned fire in forest, grass, or brush

Protecting Yourself and Your Family

Extinguishers

Each of the classes of fire requires somewhat different methods to extinguish. Your choice of extinguishers will depend on what type of fires you expect to do battle against.

Extinguishers have a numerical rating that indicates the size of the fire it can handle. The higher the number, the more fire it can handle. A well-prepared office or home will have at least two extinguishers.

There are five types of extinguishers: water, dry chemical, halon, carbon dioxide, and foam. Water and foam remove the heat. Foam also cuts off the air supply, as does carbon dioxide. Halon and dry chemical agents break the chain reaction. The special agents used against Class D fires usually remove air. Use water, foam, or dry chemical against class A fires. Use foam, carbon dioxide, dry chemical, or halon against Class B. Electrical fires should be fought with nonconductive agents (carbon dioxide, dry chemical, or halon).

To use a portable extinguisher, follow the instructions shown on it. The basic method is:

- **PULL** the pin
- **AIM** the nozzle
- **SQUEEZE** the handle
- **SWEEP** the base of the fire

In the United States extinguishers are everywhere. In most other parts of the world a bucket of water or dirt (or sand) is still the main "extinguisher."

Extinguishers and alarms.

Example of an extinguisher rating.

Alarms

Smoke alarms detect smoke and sound an alarm. Smoke alarms are cheap, and if you can't afford one you can probably get one free from your local fire department, health department, or emergency management office. If you have alarms in your home that run on house current, remember that they will not work when the power is out. Supplement them with a couple of battery-operated units. Have a smoke alarm on every level of the structure. Test them monthly and change the batteries at least once per year.

A battery-operated carbon monoxide alarm is also a good investment. Place one near the sleeping area, and if you have a designated safe room or shelter area, place one near there. Carbon monoxide is a by-product of inefficient combustion and replaces oxygen. Simply put, carbon monoxide molecules take all the oxygen parking places, and oxygen has no place to park. Any fire or fuel-burning device produces carbon monoxide.

Gas detectors are available and can be placed near the furnace and hot water heater. Test the device monthly.

Sprinkler Systems

For most of us, a sprinkler system in the home is not in our budget. For business the investment could be more worthwhile. Sprinkler systems detect heat and respond to it by spraying water from a sprinkler head.

Making a Decision to Fight a Structure Fire

In a wide-spread disaster, calling the fire department will be low on the list of priorities. Evacuate the structure first. Then make your decision about whether to fight the fire. Ask yourself these three questions: Will I be able to escape quickly if I stay to fight it and something goes wrong? Do I have the correct equipment and enough of it for the type and size of fire? Is the area free from other dangers, such as hazardous material, structural collapse? If the answer to any of these questions is no, leave immediately. Do NOT attempt to fight the fire. Shut doors behind you to contain the fire.

If You Attempt to Fight the Fire

• Wear safety equipment including helmet, goggles, dust mask, gloves, and boots.

• Work with a partner, and have a backup team standing by.

• Have two ways to get out of the fire area.

• Feel closed doors with the back of the hand, from the bottom up. Fire will be behind a hot door.

• Keep doors closed to confine the fire.

• Always worry about carbon monoxide, heated air, and toxic fire gases. Do not wear a respirator mask into an oxygen depleted atmosphere.

• Stay low to the ground. Smoke and heat will concentrate higher in the room.

• If it can be done without increasing the size of the fire, open windows for ventilation to remove smoke. Try to cross ventilate by opening windows on opposite sides of the room, or placing a fan blowing in and a fan blowing out.

• Keep a safe distance from the fire.

• Remove heat by cooling. This means using water in class A fires (typical structure fires).

• If there's an interior wet standpipe in your building, use three people to operate it: one to handle the hose, one to bleed air from the lines, and one to control the water pressure. Most interior wet standpipes will have a hundred feet of jacketed hose with a three-eighths-inch nozzle tip, using up to 125 gallons per minute. That's a lot of pressure. Hang on tightly and get a good stance before opening the nozzle.

If Inside During a Fire

- Stay low to the floor and exit the building as quickly as possible.
- Cover your nose and mouth with a wet cloth.
- When approaching a closed door, use the back of your hand to feel the lower, middle, and upper parts of the door. Never use the palm of your hand or fingers to test for heat: burning those areas could impair your ability to escape a fire (i.e., ladders and crawling).
- If the door is NOT hot, open slowly and ensure fire and/or smoke is not blocking your escape route. If your escape route is blocked, shut the door immediately and use an alternate escape route, such as a window. If clear, leave immediately through the door. Be prepared to crawl. Smoke and heat rise. The air is clearer and cooler near the floor.
- If the door is hot, do not open it. Escape through a window. If you cannot escape, hang a white or light-colored sheet outside the window, alerting firefighters to your presence.
- Heavy smoke and poisonous gases collect first along the ceiling. Stay below the smoke at all times.

Wildfires

Minimize wildfire losses by doing some pre-event preparation:

- Use fire resistant building material. Build to code.
- Build roads and driveways at least 16 feet wide.
- Maintain at least two exits in the home.
- Keep your chimney clean.
- Don't burn openly in dry weather.
- Maintain some clean space:

- Keep drains and gutters free from vegetation.
- Put a non-flammable screen over flues.
- Remove all vegetation within ten feet of any stove or chimney.
- Soak fireplace ashes and charcoal in water before disposing of it.
- Widely space landscape vegetation.
- Remove branches to a height of 15 feet.
- Maintain a fuel-free zone around all structures for a minimum of 30 feet—remove dry and excess vegetation, garbage, and any sources of tinder.
- Store propane tanks at a significant distance from buildings and maintain a fuel-free zone around them.
- Store combustibles such as firewood away from buildings.

- Leave a 100-foot garden hose connected to a freeze-proof faucet, and leave a ladder long enough to reach the roof nearby.
- Have firefighting tools handy: ladder, shovels, rakes, buckets.
- Clearly mark your address and road signs so firefighters can find your property if called.

During a Wildfire

- Listen to the media for information and instructions.
- Remove any combustibles (lawn furniture, etc.) from around the house.
- Remove flammable drapes and blinds.
- Close doors and windows.
- Close gas valves and turn off pilot lights.

- Turn on every light when needed for visibility in dense smoke.
- Put large waterproof valuables into a pool or pond.
- Leave sprinklers on, aimed at the roof and the side of the house facing the approaching fire.
- Be ready to get out fast.
- If smoke gets dense before you can evacuate, stay low to get the best air.
- If you are overcome by fire, get low or float face up in a pond or stream. Cover the head and upper chest with wet clothing. If no body of water is available, get into the large boulders, or lie flat and cover yourself with wet clothing or soil.

After the Fire

- Take great caution, hot spots can smolder for hours before flaring up.
- Check and recheck the roof and walls, then wait a few hours and check again. Get a distant look at the building to see smoke from any lingering hotspots.

4. Flood

The Basics

A flood is an abnormal expanse of water that submerges land. It occurs when the water exceeds its normal depth or it flows above or beyond the normal limits of its container.

Floods of seawater can be caused by heavy storms, high tides, and tsunamis. Seawater flooding from storm surges often combines with intense monsoon or tropical storm rains to produce devastating floods. Seawater floods are particularly devastating because of the large populations concentrated on coastlines and the long-term salt damage to farmland soils.

River flooding may occur because of heavy storms, high runoff, and sometimes due to high temperatures causing accelerated melting of the snowpack. The river overflows its banks onto the flood plain. Flash floods are often the result of intense rainfall in a particular drainage or system of drainages. The factors in a flashflood include slope, drainage, vegetation, soil and surface conditions, and saturation. Flash floods can move slowly and hit hours later when the sun is shining.

Floods can also be caused by blocked waterways. The blockages can be ice and debris jams on rivers, or clogged sewers and community water systems.

Floods are so common that flood insurance can be hard to get, and insurance companies will often find any available loophole in insurance policies to deny a flood-damage claim.

The Jargon

Dike—A low wall, ditch, or embankment.

Flash flood—A sudden flood, usually cause by a heavy rain.

Flood plain—A low plain next to a river, formed of river sediment and subject to flooding.

Flash Flood Watch—Flash flooding is possible. Tune to NOAA weather radio of other media for information.

Flash Flood Warning—A flash flood is occurring. Seek higher ground on foot immediately.

Flood Watch—Flooding is possible. Tune to NOAA weather radio or other media for information.

Flood Warning—Flooding is occurring or will occur soon. If advised to evacuate, do so immediately.

Monsoon—Seasonal wind system or the rain that accompanies that wind.

Precipitation—Solid or liquid water that falls from the air to the earth.

Storm surge—A local rise in sea level near the shore caused by strong winds from a storm.

Tide—Rise and fall of the sea happening twice each lunar day.

Tsunami—An ocean wave produced by submarine earthquake, volcano, or landslide

Protecting Yourself and Your Family

Preparing

- Find out how likely floods are in your area.
- Know the local emergency plan and evacuation routes.
- Raise the furnace, water heater, and electric appliances off the floor.
- Install sump pumps and make arrangements for backup power.
- Construct barriers to deflect water around the home.
- Anchor outdoor fuel tanks.
- Get some flood insurance.

If There's Time Before an Impending Flood

- Secure the home. Move furniture and valuables upstairs.
- Turn off the utilities at the main switches or valves if instructed to do so. Unplug appliances, but don't touch electrical equipment if you're standing

in water. Don't be in water where appliances are plugged in.

- Fill your gas tank and head for high ground.

If the Flood Threat Is Immediate (A Flash Flood)

- Stay away from water courses and drainages.
- Get out of a watercourse onto high ground. If you're in a deep drainage with no escape, run like hell downstream. It will buy you some time.

Author's note: during the filming of the BBC/Discovery Channel series Planet Earth, *I chased flash floods with a camera crew for six weeks in the Southwest's slickrock canyon country. I learned that, contrary to what you are told, it is quite possible to outrun some flash floods. Running beats standing there waiting for the wall of water to swallow you up.*

- In your car, don't cross flooded roads. As little as six inches of water can push your car off.
- If you are trapped midstream, get on the car top.
- Do not wade anything above mid-calf. You risk being swept away or entrapping your foot. If you must cross a shallow but swift stream, use a stick or other people for support.
- If you MUST get into deeper swift water, swim it. Get on your back in a defensive swimming position: feet downhill, head up, steering with your arms and warding off obstacles with your feet. Angle your head toward the shore you wish to reach. This will put you at an angle that makes the current push you toward that shore (a "ferry angle").

- Never tie into a rope in moving water. It will pull you down and drown you. Do not go into the water to rescue someone. If you have a rope, throw it in small coils directly at the swimmer. If they grab it, take a strong stance and hold on. They will pendulum in toward the shore.

- For emergency flotation use anything less dense than air or that holds air. Some empty plastic bottles in a backpack make an excellent personal flotation device.

After a Flood

- Listen to the media and return when authorities say it's safe.

- Downed power lines are a hazard. Stay away from fallen lines and transformers. Report the damage to the power company.

- Floods contaminate local water supplies with oil, gasoline, and sewage. Don't play in the water. Wash your hands often and clean injuries thoroughly.

- Disinfect toys and other metal/plastic items with a 1:10 solution of bleach and water (1½ cup bleach to a gallon of water).

- Throw way any food that might have been contaminated by flood water.

5. Hurricanes and Other Cyclonic Storms

The Basics

A tropical cyclone is a storm system with a low pressure center and storms that produce high winds, tornados, heavy rain, and storm surges. These storms develop and grow over warm seas as moist warm air rises and water vapor condenses. Because of the Coriolis effect (remember that from ninth-grade earth science?), cyclones rotate counterclockwise in the Northern Hemisphere and counterclockwise in the Southern Hemisphere, and are referred to as tropical depressions, tropical storms, typhoons, cyclones, or hurricanes, depending on their location and intensity or strength.

Tropical cyclonic storms lose strength when they move over land. Coastal areas get the full brunt of the storm and suffer from the high winds, heavy rain, and storm surges, causing serious coastal flooding. Inland areas usually experience reduced winds but can still experience serious flooding from heavy rains.

The Jargon

Eye—A core of relatively calm air in the center of a hurricane.

Hurricane—A large rotating tropical weather system with winds of at least 74 miles per hour.

Hurricane categories:

Storm surge—A local rise in sea level caused by strong winds from a storm.

Hurricane/Tropical Storm Warning—Hurricane/tropical storm conditions are expected within 24 hours.

Hurricane/Tropical Storm Watch—Hurricane/tropical storm conditions are possible within 36 hours. Tune to NOAA weather radio or other media for information.

Storm Tide—A combination of normal tide and storm surge.

Tropical Storm—An organized system of strong thunderstorms with a defined circulation and maximum sustained winds of 39–73 miles per hour.

Category	Sustained wind (mph)	Damage	Storm surge
Category 1	74–95	Minimal. None to permanent structures. Some to unanchored mobile homes and vegetation.	4–5 feet
Category 2	96–110	Moderate. Roofing, door, and window damage.	6–8 feet
Category 3	111–130	Extensive. More structural damage. Mobile homes destroyed. Some structural damage from flooding on the coast.	9–12 feet
Category 4	131–155	Extreme. Extensive damage. Beach erosion. Trees down. Inland flooding.	13–18 feet
Category 5	>155	Catastrophic. Complete roof or building failure of many structures. Major roads cut off. Major flood damage near the shore. Mass evacuations likely.	>18 feet

Hurricane Categories and Characteristics

Protecting Yourself and Your Family

Before the Storm

- Know the local risks, evacuation routes, and shelter locations.
- Take in outdoor items, including furniture and awnings. Tie down large objects. Cut down and dispose of dead branches and any live branches that are too close to the house.
- Close and secure window shutters, or cover windows with plywood or boards.
- Check your disaster supply kit to make sure the radio and lights work and the batteries are fresh.
- Lock all doors and windows to reduce vibration. Close drapes and curtains, and tape windows to limit and contain flying glass.
- Tie/anchor down mobile homes.
- Review your insurance policy.
- Fill the car with gas and prepare to evacuate.
- Listen to the NOAA weather radio or other media for information.
- If told to evacuate, go immediately.

During the Storm

- Stay indoors and away from windows. Go to your safe room if you have one.
- Stay away from flood waters.
- Be alert for tornadoes.
- Remember, the "eye" of the storm means the storm is only half over.

After the Storm

- Listen to the media for information.
- Wait until the area is declared safe before entering.
- Use a flashlight to inspect for damage, including gas, water, electrical lines, and appliances.
- If you smell gas or fire, turn off the gas main. Switch off individual circuit breakers (or unscrew individual fuses) and turn off the main breaker (or unscrew the main fuse).
- Stay away from downed power lines.
- Use the phone for urgent calls only.
- If the area has flooded, drink the local water only if it has been declared safe. Throw out any food contaminated by flood waters.

6.   Tornadoes

The Basics

A tornado is a violent column of rotating air formed when a warm humid air mass meets a cold air mass. The column, or condensation funnel cloud, is usually in contact with a cumulonimbus cloud base above and the ground below. The bottom of the funnel is usually surrounded by a debris cloud. Tornados occur most often in the United States, but do occur elsewhere. A tornado over water is called a waterspout. Tornados move at an average speed of 30 miles per hour, but can move twice or half that speed. The internal winds can reach 300 miles per hour. The path of damage can be miles long and hundreds of feet wide.

Tornados are rated by the Fuijita (F) Scale or the Enhanced Fijita Scale (EF) according to the damage they cause. An F0 causes light damage and can strip some tree limbs off, but won't seriously damage structures. An F5 will cause incredible damage and will tear a building off its foundation. Tornados can strike without warning and can travel fast, changing directions with no warning. Knowing the potential F rating isn't important. If you hear the warning or see the funnel, take appropriate action.

The signs of a tornado are:

- A funnel cloud, sometimes difficult to see
- Dark sky with an eerie greenish tone
- Large dark low-lying clouds
- High winds becoming calm or still
- Loud roar, "like a freight train"

The Jargon

Cumulonimbus—A cumulus cloud that produces thunderstorms.

Funnel cloud—A rotating column of air working its way down from the bottom of a cumulonimbus cloud.

Water spout—A tornado over a large body of water.

Dust devil—A circular wind that picks up dust, not associated with a tornado.

Fujita scale—A scale defining tornado intensity and damage.

Tornado Warning—A tornado has been sighted or indicated by weather radar. Take shelter immediately.

Tornado Watch—Tornadoes are possible. Remain alert for approaching storms. Watch the sky and monitor NOAA weather radio or other media for information.

Protecting Yourself and Your Family

Before Tornado Season

- Find or make a low, windowless, structurally sound place to take shelter in. Consider the basement, under the stairs, a safe room, or an interior hallway or closet on the lowest floor.
- Find or make a low, windowless, structurally strong place to take shelter in. Consider the basement, under stairs, a safe room, an interior hallway or closet on the lowest floor.
- If your house is a mobile home, configure it with a tie-down system to limit damage, but avoid using it for shelter.
- Learn the siren signals in your area.
- Do drills with the family.

When a Tornado Is Imminent

- Take cover immediately. Most injuries are caused by flying debris.
- Report sighted tornadoes.
- Stay away from windows to avoid airborne glass shards.
- Go to your designated shelter or to the interior part of the basement or an interior room on the lowest floor. Avoid being near doors, windows, outside walls, and corners. Do not stay directly beneath heavy furniture or appliances on the floor above.
- Get under a heavy table or other sturdy cover. Cover yourself with a mattress or heavy blankets. Cover and protect you head and face.

- If you're in a mobile home, go to the community tornado shelter. If there is none or you don't have time, go to a sturdy nearby building, to the basement or an interior room on the lowest floor. If that's not possible, get out of the mobile home and lie flat in the nearest ground depression, preferably a ditch or culvert.
- If you're in a vehicle:
    - Stop and get out.
    - Get in a nearby ditch or low spot.
    - Never get under the car. Stay away from vehicles.
    - Protect your head under structural cover or with your arms.
    - Avoid areas with trees.
- If you're in a building other than your home:
    - Take the precautions given above.
    - Avoid elevators.
- If you're in a mall or large gymnasium:
    - Stay away from windows and glass doors.
    - Get to the lowest level.
    - Get under a door frame or huddle against a structure that will deflect falling debris.

After a Tornado

- Enter a building only after authorities have checked the foundation for shifting or cracking and the walls and ceilings for structural soundness.
- If you smell gas, shut off the main valve immediately and call the gas company.
- Shut off the electricity and have an electrician check for circuit shorts.

7.   Winter Storms

The Basics

Winter storms are weather disturbances that combine cold temperatures with the resulting forms of precipitation (snow, sleet, ice, freezing rain). These are usually winter events, but can often occur in spring and fall. In this section we focus on the effects of precipitation or the combined effects of precipitation and cold. For heat and cold emergencies, see the next section.

Winter storms can wreak havoc:

- Disrupted traffic and increased risk of accidents due to limited visibility, icy roads, deep drifts
- Disruption in transportation and distribution of goods and supplies, resulting in depletions of food, water, and medical supplies for humans and livestock
- Cut-off of emergency response teams
- Increased risk of cold injuries (frostbite and hypothermia, exertion injuries and illnesses, and carbon monoxide poisoning)
- Structural collapse, including buildings and power lines, due to deep or heavy wet snow
- Avalanches in mountainous areas (common in Alaska, Colorado, Utah and some other mountain states)
- Flooding in low lying areas

The Jargon

Avalanche—A slide of large masses of snow or ice down a mountain slope.
Avalanche Warning—A forecast to draw attention to severe avalanche danger.

Blizzard Scale—A blizzard has winds of 35–44 miles per hour and visibility less than 500 feet. A severe blizzard has winds over 45 miles per hour and zero visibility.

Blizzard Warning—Sustained winds or gusts to 35 miles per hour or greater and considerable falling or blowing snow expected for a period of three hours or longer.

Freezing Rain—Rain that freezes when it hits the ground.

Frost or Freeze Warning—Below freezing temperatures are expected.

Heavy Snow Warning—A significant amount of snow is forecast that will make travel dangerous.

Sleet—Rain that turns to ice before it hits the ground

Travel Advisory—Weather conditions have created impassable or hazardous roads.

Wind Chill—The reason why it feels colder when the wind blows. A product of wind speed and air temperature.

Winter Storm Warning—A significant winter storm or hazardous winter weather is occurring, imminent, or likely and is a threat to life and property.

Winter Storm Watch—Significant winter weather is expected within 12 to 36 hours.

Protecting Yourself and Your Family

Before the Storm

- General preparations for winter should include draining water from sprinkler lines, draining outdoor hoses, closing inside valves that supply outdoor hose faucets, and opening outside valves to drain water and allow ice to expand.
- Protect pipes with insulating sleeves or heat tape.
- Insulate the walls and attic.

- Clean out rain gutters to allow runoff and keep them from blocking with snow and ice.
- Prepare for power loss. Maintain a disaster supply kit. Maintain a reasonable supply of heating fuel.
- Winterize your home by repairing roof damage and blocking small holes in the walls and around pipes and vents. Maintain weather-stripping around windows and doors.
- Check batteries in smoke and carbon monoxide detectors.
- Have a professional clean your furnace, flues, and chimney.
- Maintain snow removal equipment.
- Winterize your car:
    - Keep the tank full.
    - Check your battery and clean the terminals.
    - Check antifreeze levels and the thermostat.
    - Check the heater, defroster, windshield wipers, and add windshield washer fluid.
    - Check the exhaust system.
    - Change to a lightweight oil.
    - Install all-weather radials or snow tires.
    - Keep an ice scraper and a broom in the car.
    - Carry an emergency car kit.

During a Storm

- Put on warm clothes.
- Protect water pipes with insulation or an external heat source. Allow water to trickle from faucets to prevent freezing.
- Do not allow drinking water to freeze.

In the Car

- Drive only if absolutely necessary and only during the day.
- Stay on the main roads.
- Travel with a companion.
- Tell someone your destination, schedule, and route.
- Take along a cell phone or a two-way radio.
- If trapped by a blizzard:
    - Pull off and turn on the hazard lights or tie a bright tape or cloth to the antenna or window. Raising the hood may signal distress, but you'll lose engine heat.
    - Open a downwind window slightly for ventilation.
    - Operate the engine and heater for only 10 minutes per hour to prevent carbon monoxide poisoning. Occasionally clear snow from the exhaust.
    - Leave an overhead light on only when the engine is running.
    - Insulate as much as possible and huddle together.
    - Change position frequently and move around to generate body warmth and avoid cramps.
    - Take turns staying awake on safety watch.
    - Drink fluids to avoid dehydration. Avoid eating snow or ice. It lowers body temperature.
    - When the storm clears, if you are stranded, stomp an SOS into deep snow, or burn engine oil for a smoke and fire signal.

After a Storm

- Listen to media for information and forecasts.
- Check the Internet and telephone resources for road conditions.
- Check on your neighbors, especially anyone with special needs.

8.   Thunderstorms & Lightning

The Basics

All thunderstorms and lightning are dangerous. Many people are killed by lightning and the survivors of lightning strikes can suffer a variety of long-term complications. Thunderstorms can be dry or wet and are associated with tornadoes, strong winds, and flash floods.

The Jargon

Severe Thunderstorm Watch—Severe thunderstorms are likely to occur. Watch the sky and listen to NOAA weather radio or other media for information.

Severe Thunderstorm Warning—Severe weather has been reported by spotters or indicated by radar. There is imminent danger to life and property for those in the path of the storm.

Protecting Yourself and Your Family

- The 30/30 lightning safety rule: If after seeing lightning you cannot count to 30 before hearing thunder, get inside a building or an automobile (not a convertible). Stay indoors for 30 minutes after hearing the last thunder.

- Delay outdoor activities.
- Don't shower or bathe during the storm. Pipes and fixtures can conduct electrical current.
- Use your cell phone, but not your landline (POTS telephone line).
- Lightning can cause power surges. Turn off electronics and appliances.
- Monitor NOAA weather radio and other media for information.
- Avoid tall isolated trees, hilltops, beaches, open water, open fields, small isolated sheds in open areas, and anything metal.
- If in a forest, get low under a thick stand of small trees.
- If in open terrain, go to a gully or ravine. Be watchful for flash flooding.
- If on the water, get to land and find shelter.
- If you feel your hair standing or hear metal buzzing, crouch low to the ground but do not lie flat.

After the Storm

- If anyone is injured, check ABCs and seek medical help.

9. Cold & Heat Emergencies

The Basics

Here we're talking about cold waves and heat waves or unique events when the temperature is acutely and extremely colder or hotter than usual for the average climate of a region. Heat and cold waves are prolonged periods of excessively hot or cold temperature. Both conditions can be exacerbated by humidity, although it's more often a factor in heat waves. They both have common effects:

- Crop failures due to cooking or freezing of vulnerable plants.
- Deaths by hypothermia or hyperthermia ("exposure" and heat stroke), especially among the elderly, chronically ill, and homeless. Also, in the case of cold waves, there's an increase in carbon monoxide poisoning from the extensive use of fuel-burning heaters.
- Illnesses related to dehydration.
- Power outages due to increased use of heating or air conditioning.
- Structural damage, especially roads, from expansion and contraction.
- Wildfires during heat waves and structural fires during cold waves.

See Chapter 5 (Emergency Heating and Cooling) and Chapter 9 (First Aid and Light Rescue) for more detailed information on those particular aspects of heat and cold emergencies.

The Jargon

Dehydration—A condition in which the loss of body fluids exceeds the amount taken in.

Frostbite—Damage to skin and other tissues due to extreme cold.

Heat exhaustion—When the body is too hot, either from exercise or weather. The body's cooling system is still working but not keeping up.

Heat stroke—A medical emergency in which the body's cooling system has stopped working.

Hypothermia—A condition in which the body temperature falls below 95 degrees because more heat is being lost than gained.

	Heat Wave	Cold Wave
Activity	Avoid strenuous activity. Work during the coolest parts of the day.	Do not avoid strenuous activity, except to maintain energy levels during food and water deficiencies. Get in bed to maintain warmth during the coldest part of the day.
Shelter	Move to the lowest level of the building, where cool air falls.	Move to the upper level of the building, where warm air rises.
Clothing	Strip down indoors. Outdoors, cover up with long sleeves and pants to reduce sunburn. Light colors are significantly cooler than dark in the sunlight. Moist clothing can provide a swamp-cooler effect in low-humidity heat.	Dress in layers: a weather resistant shell over insulation. Wear a hat. Cover the mouth. Stay dry or change out of wet clothes. Wear mittens.
Food and Nutrition	Drink plenty of water.	Drink plenty of water. Eat lots of carbohydrates.
Pre-Disaster Preparation	See chapter 5	See chapter 5

Protecting Yourself and Your Family

A summary of protective measures:

10. Earthquake

The Basics

In a nutshell, an earthquake is a ground-shake that usually only lasts a few seconds. Strong earthquakes can cause massive structural damage and a high death toll. The after-effects can include massive urban fires and giant killer ocean waves (tsunamis).

Earthquakes are caused by the movement of faults generated by the constant motion of tectonic plates. Earthquakes are most common in areas along the edges of tectonic plates (California, Japan, etc.). In the United States, strong earthquakes are most common in Alaska, Hawaii, the West Coast, and the intermountain states (Nevada, Idaho, Wyoming, Montana, and Utah), although other areas of the country, such as the central Mississippi Valley, are also at risk.

Quakes send seismic waves through the ground that can be measured all over the world. The strength and intensity of earthquakes are measured using the Richter Scale and the Modified Mercali Scale.

The Jargon

Earthquake-proofing—Modifying a structure and its contents to withstand the effects of an earthquake.
Epicenter—The surface location directly above the center of the earthquake.

Richter Scale—A scale, 1–10, used to measure the energy (magnitude) of an earthquake.

Modified Mecalli Scale—A scale of earthquake intensity measuring the severity of shaking. A scale-1 earthquake is weak, causing no damage. A scale-12 is a quake causing nearly total destruction.

Tectonic plates—Plates of the earth's outer shell in relative motion to one another.

Fault—A break in the earth's crust along which movement can take place, causing an earthquake.

Seismic waves—Waves caused by earthquakes.

Liquefaction—A process by which saturated soil behaves like liquid during an earthquake, with devastating effect on structures.

Aftershock—A weaker earthquake in the same area as the main earthquake.

Protecting Yourself and Your Family

Before the Quake

- Make structural modifications, including extra bracing and sill plate/foundation bolts, or hold-downs to secure walls to foundations. Strap the chimney in place with structural straps and angle bracing.
- Repair defective wiring. Install flexible utility connections.
- Secure fuel oil and propane tanks to the floor or ground and install flexible connections.
- Secure the fridge, furnace, and heavy appliances to wall studs with heavy strapping.
- Secure the water heater with heavy strapping or metal plumber's tape.

- Store large heavy objects and breakables on lower shelves.
- Reinforce attachments of overhead light fixtures and ceiling fans.
- Secure mirrors, shelves, and frames to the walls.
- Choose an alternate exit from each room.
- Do practice drills with the family and coworkers.

During the Quake

- Most injuries are caused by debris from collapsing structures and falling objects.
- Get under a strong doorway, against an inside wall, in a safe room, or under stable, heavy furniture such as a bed or desk.
- If in bed, stay in bed until the shaking stops.
- Avoid being near windows, outside doors, or weak walls.
- Stay inside until the shaking stops.
- If you are outdoors:
  - Stay put until the shaking stops. Crouch and protect your head and face with your arms.
  - Move away from buildings, fuel tanks, and power lines.
  - Don't go into nearby buildings.
- If you are in a vehicle:
  - Pull over and stop away from utility poles, trees, wires, overpasses, and fuel tanks.
  - Set the emergency brake.
  - Stay in the vehicle.
- If you are trapped under rubble:

- Make an airspace (a void) where you can breath.
- Do not use matches or lighters.
- Keep still to avoid kicking up and breathing dust.
- Cover your mouth and nose with clothing or a handkerchief.
- Signal by tapping on a pipe or wall.

After the Quake

- Expect aftershocks.
- Be alert to the possibility of flooding and tsunamis. If in a low area near a large body of water, head for higher ground (for instance, in the "big one" expected along the Wasatch Fault, some experts predict the Great Salt Lake will tilt and splash up against the west slope of the Wasatch Mountains, killing thousands). Liquefaction and damage to dams may also increase the risk of local flooding. In coastal areas, tsunamis are possible. Get to higher ground.
- Enter damaged buildings as carefully as possible, preferably after authorities have inspected the foundation for shifting and the walls and ceilings for structural soundness.
- If there is structural damage or you smell gas, shut off the main gas valve.
- Shut off the electricity and have your circuits checked for shorts.
- Listen to the media for information and instructions.
- Stay away from downed power lines.
- In the home:

- Shut off the main water valve if the pipes are damaged.
- If you smell gas, get out. If you haven't already, shut of the gas main. Report leaks to the gas company or authorities.
- Check the sewage lines for damage before using the toilet.
- Open cabinets cautiously.
- Clean up spilled flammables.
- When possible, have a professional check the house for structural damage.
- Be prepared to evacuate.

11.   Landslides & Mass Wasting

The Basics

Landslides are down-slope movement of rock, soil, or related debris. Landslides are synonymous with the term "mass wasting," a variety of processes such as rock fall, creep, slump, mudflow, earth flow, and debris flow. In most mass wasting, water plays a key role by assisting in the decomposition and loosening of rock, lubricating rock and soil surfaces, adding weight to the soil, and giving buoyancy to the individual particles. This material will remain stationary until it exceeds its angle of repose and starts to slide. The proportions of rock, sand, clay, and water will dictate the type of slope failure, speed, and extent of a slide.

Landslides are propelled by gravity but they are often set off by other natural disasters, like volcanoes and earthquakes, or by human activity. A type of debris flow called "lahar"—

a mixture of volcanic ash and water—is specific to volcanic activity. Lahars are often the major hazard experienced in a volcanic event. Although earthquakes can initiate debris flows, the major causes of landslides in the United States are rains that saturate soils.

Landslides often result directly from human activity. Modifications of surface flow and drainage can lead to landslides, as is the case in most urban landslides. Construction too close to eroding shores and vista points can lead to the loss of a structure. Over-irrigation, clear cutting, clearing vegetation by human or wildfire causes, and highway construction, especially highway cuts, can result in a landslide hazard.

Many unstable areas can be recognized from scarps, tilted and bent trees, wetlands and standing water, irregular and hummocky ground topography, over-steepened slopes with a thick soil cover, or steep slopes that have been burned clean. Mass movement can often be seen in aerial photography.

The Jargon

Angle of repose—the steepest angle that allows a material to be stationary.

Lahar—a debris flow of volcanic ash and water.

Mass wasting—the downhill movement of rock and soil under the direct influence of gravity.

Mudflow—a debris flow containing large amounts of water that usually occurs in canyons and gullies of mountainous areas.

Slump—a slide along a curved surface where unconsolidated material slips downward as a unit.

Rockslide—slide of a rock mass along planes of weakness.

Protecting Yourself and Your Family

Before a Slide

- Find out if you area has a history of slides or is considered at risk for slides by contacting the USGS, local emergency management, or the geology departments at nearby universities and colleges.
- Check the drainage patterns above your house. Watch for changes. Look for signs of ground movement. Poles and trees that lean past vertical uphill are a bad sign.
- Check and update your insurance policy.

During Wet Periods

- Listen to the NOAA weather radio and other media for information and warnings.
- Flash floods and mud flows may produce a characteristic apron of water or thin mud in front of the flow that tends to raise the level of water in front of it. If the stream rises or you detect a shallow mud flow, be suspicious and take precautions. Most streams go dirty brown during storms, so color isn't a reliable indicator when it's raining.
- Listen for unusual noises. Look for recently upslope-tilted utility poles and trees.
- Consider evacuating or moving to an upper story if you become suspicious. Be prepared to move quickly. Mud flows and flash floods can travel over 30 miles per hour.
- If you detect a debris flow, get out of its path to high ground as fast as possible.
- If caught in the flow, curl into a tight ball and cover your head.

After the Slide

- Stay away from the slide area. Stay out of the direct slide path. More slides are possible.
- Scan the area for victims and make notes of where they might be. Give the information to rescuers when they arrive.
- Report downed power lines and any other hazards you see.

12. Tsunami

A tsunami is a series of waves that occur when a large body of water is suddenly displaced on a massive scale. Tectonic causes such as earthquakes and volcanoes are often thought of as the primary origins of tsunamis, but massive landslides, ice shelf collapse, and even nuclear weapons and meteor and asteroid impacts could cause a tsunami.

An earthquake is usually the first warning of an impending tsunami. Tsunamis can pass unnoticed in the deep ocean, traveling as fast as 450 miles per hour, but as they approach land a trough, rather than a wave crest, develops and water along the shoreline recedes and exposes areas that are normally submerged. The crest usually arrives very shortly after (seconds or minutes).

Hawaii and Alaska see more tsunamis than anywhere else in the United States, although the entire West Coast is at risk. Tsunami Warning Centers in Hawaii and Alaska use a buoy monitor system to detect disturbances that might indicate a tsunami. When a tsunami is recorded, the center tracks it and issues a warning when needed.

Drowning is the most common cause of death associated with a tsunami, and the waves and the receding water are very destructive to structures. Secondary hazards include flooding, salt contamination of farming soil, contamination of drinking water, and fires from gas lines or ruptured tanks.

The Jargon

Tsunami Advisory—An earthquake has occurred and might generate a tsunami.

Tsunami Warning—A dangerous tsunami was or could have been generated and people in the warning area are strongly advised to evacuate.

Tsunami Watch—A dangerous tsunami may have been generated but it is at least two hours away from the watch area.

How to Protect Yourself and Your Family

Before and During a Tsunami

- Turn on your radio to learn if there is a tsunami warning if an earthquake occurs and you are in a coastal area.
- Move inland to higher ground immediately and stay there.
- Stay away from the beach. Never go down to the beach to watch a tsunami come in. If you can see the wave you are too close to escape it. If there is noticeable recession in water away from the shoreline you should move away immediately.

After the Tsunami

- Monitor the media for information and instructions.

- Stay away from flooded and damaged areas until officials say it is safe to return.

- Stay away from debris in the water; it may pose a safety hazard to boats and people.

13. Volcano

The Basics

A volcano is an opening to a pool of molten rock below the surface of the earth. When pressure builds up, eruptions occur. Gases and molten rock shoot up through the opening and spill over or fill the air with lava fragments. Eruptions can cause lateral blasts, lava flows, hot ash flows, mudslides, avalanches, falling ash, and floods. Volcano eruptions have been known to knock down entire forests. An erupting volcano can trigger tsunamis, flash floods, earthquakes, mudflows and rockfalls.

Volcanoes usually form where tectonic plates pull apart from each other or converge with each other. They also form over hotspots away from the edges of the tectonic plates (e.g., the Hawaiian volcanoes). Active volcanoes in the U.S. are found mainly in Hawaii, Alaska, California, Oregon, and Washington.

Volcanoes can be feisty. Buildings are destroyed and people are killed or made homeless. Fresh volcanic ash, made of pulverized rock, can be harsh, acidic, gritty, glassy, and smelly. Clouds of ash cover plants making them inedible. The ash can cause acute and chronic respiratory problems. Poisonous gases like carbon dioxide and sulfur dioxide kill people and animals. Dark skies, cold temperatures, severe winds, and heavy rains may follow an eruption for months afterward, causing famine and contributing to disease. Volcanic gases may contribute to the greenhouse effect. For a good primer on volcanoes, get a copy of the movie *Dante's Peak*. In spite of a few Hollywood moments, it's a fairly accurate depiction of what can happen.

The Jargon

Active—Erupting.

Ash—Fine particles of pulverized rock.

Bomb—A large fragment of semi-molten rock hurled from an eruption.

Dormant—Inactive but may erupt in the future.

Eruption—The process by which material is ejected from a volcano.

Lava—Magma which has reached the surface through a volcanic opening.

Pyroclastic flow—The flow of a mixture of hot gases, ash, and rock fragments that can flow of speeds up to 100 miles per hour.

Protecting Yourself and Your Family

Before an Eruption

- It's likely that there will be some advanced warning from obvious activity and geologic investigation.
- Monitor local radio and TV for information and warnings.

- In volcano areas, your disaster supplies kit should include goggles and a supply of face masks. N95 respirator masks are preferred but may clog quickly. Have some simple masks on hand.

During Volcanic Activity

- Follow the advice of local authorities. Evacuate immediately if ordered to do so. Sheltering near the volcano is dangerous.
- Avoid low-lying areas where poisonous gases can accumulate.
- Avoid streambeds where mudflows are possible.
- Bring pets and livestock into closed shelters.
- If you don't have a mask, improvise one from damp cloth.
- Wear protective clothing, including a helmet if you have one.
- If stranded in an area with a heavy accumulation of ash, stay inside and keep all doors and windows closed. Turn off all fans, heating, and air conditioning systems.
- Avoid driving in heavy ashfall. Engines clog, vehicles stall, and low visibility causes accidents.
- For an ash flow or a pyroclastic flow you may have few choices. Either shelter in an underground emergency refuge or hold your breath and submerge yourself underwater as long as possible in a river, a lake, or the sea. Chances are you'll cook anyway, but there's a slim chance the danger will pass in less than a minute.

After an Earthquake

- Listen to media for information and instructions.

- Drink bottled or stored water until the local water can be tested.
- Clear the roof of ash. Ash is heavy and can cause a structural collapse.

14.   Emerging Infectious Diseases & Bioterrorism

The Basics

Emerging infections are those that have recently appeared or those whose occurrence or geographic range is quickly increasing or threatening to increase. They can be caused by previously unknown pathogens, known pathogens that have spread to new locations or new populations, or re-emerging pathogens.

The factors in the emergence or re-emergence of infectious diseases can include natural processes related to the evolution of the pathogen, or the direct results of human behavior. Population growth, urbanization, international air travel, poverty, war, and environmental excesses can all contribute.

For an emerging infectious disease to flourish it must have a vulnerable population and the ability to spread easily from person to person. Many of these diseases take root when they pass from animals to humans. Examples of this are HIV and influenza.

Another critical factor in the re-emergence of infectious diseases is acquired resistance to antibiotics and antivirals. We've seen this with TB, STDs and other infections in the last couple of decades, and scientists expect it to get worse.

Bioterrorism agents are pathogens and related toxins that are used to cause death and disease in animals (including humans) and plants for terrorist purposes. These are usually "germs" that are found in nature but modified to increase their virulence, to make them resistant to antibiotics or vaccines, or to enhance the ability of the germ to spread through the environment and from person to person.

Terrorists have an interest in biological weapons because they are cheap and accessible. They can be easily produced and delivered without detection. Most bio agents have an incubation period. They can cause public chaos and panic without the terrorist even having to be present.

Pathogens and toxins that could be used as bioterrorism agents are classified into Class A, B, and C based on their ability to be disseminated, their mortality rates, their likelihood to cause public panic, and the actions that must be taken to combat them.

Category A agents are considered the worst (or the best, from a terrorist's point of view) because they can be easily disseminated or transmitted from person to person and pose the highest risk to national security because of their high mortality rates, their potential to cause panic, and the complications of controlling their spread. They have been studied by some countries for use in biological warfare and include anthrax, botulism, plague, smallpox, Tularemia, and viral hemorrhagic fevers like ebola and marburg.

Category C includes germs that could be engineered for dissemination, and also includes some agents that are currently considered emerging infection threats, like SARS and drug resistant TB.

Bio weapons can be delivered by wet or dry aerosol sprays, by explosive devices, by vectors and direct contact with carriers, by introduction into our food and water, contamination of medications, or by contact with germ-laden objects.

The Jargon

Antibiotic—A substance that can destroy or inhibit the growth of microorganisms.

Antiviral—A substance that can destroy or inhibit the growth of viruses.

Bioterrorism agents—Pathogens and toxins that may be used for bioterrorism.

Contagious disease—Infectious disease that can be caught by a person who comes in contact with someone who is infected.

Contaminate—To make impure or unclean by contact.

Disinfection—To cleanse so as to destroy "germs".

Dissemination—To spread around or abroad.

Eradication—To eliminate completely.

Infectious disease—Diseases caused by the invasion of harmful organisms.

Incubation period—The time from exposure to a germ to the time the patient begins to have symptoms.

Isolation—Removes people who are ill with contagious diseases from the general public.

Microorganism—Microscopic organisms that may or may not cause disease.

Mortality rate—Ratio of deaths to a population.

Pandemic—Widespread epidemic disease.

Pathogens—An agent that causes disease, including bacteria, viruses, and parasites—germs.

Quarantine—Separates people who may have been exposed to a contagious disease but who are not yet ill.

Toxin—A poisonous substance produced from microorganisms.

Vaccine—A preparation of a weakened or dead pathogen that stimulates antibody production but doesn't cause disease.

Vector—An organism that carries disease-causing germs from one organism to another.

Virulence—The capacity of a germ to cause disease.

Zoonosis—A disease of animals that can be transmitted to humans.

Protecting Yourself and Your Family

There has been a lot of barely justifiable public and government paranoia about bioterrorism and emerging infections. A pandemic is a horrible concept in terms of the death toll. In modern times we've fed that fear with an endless stream of *Dawn of the Dead* and *Andromeda Strain*-style movies. Let's get realistic and practical about all of this. Biological warfare and emerging infections are nothing more than infectious diseases, and there are standard, common ways of reducing the chance that you'll be a victim of either:

- **Wash your hands often**, especially before and after preparing food, before eating and after using the toilet.
- **Get vaccinated**. Keep your and your children's vaccinations up to date. If you travel, get the recommended vaccines for your destination.

- **Use antibiotics and antivirals only when needed**. Take them exactly as directed. Don't stop taking them early because you feel better.

- **Stay at home if you feel sick or have cold symptoms**. Don't go to work with nausea, diarrhea, or a fever. Don't send your children to school if they have these symptoms.

- **Prepare food properly**. Keep counters and other kitchen surfaces clean. Promptly refrigerate leftovers.

- **Disinfect the "germiest" areas of your home**—the kitchen and bathroom.

- **Practice safe sex**.

- **Don't share** toothbrushes, combs, razor blades, towels, drinking glasses, or eating utensils.

- **Be a smart and courteous traveler**. Nobody wants to share the cabin of a plane or a ride in a taxi with somebody who's sick.

- **Keep your pets healthy**. Practice good pet nutrition and hygiene. Keep them up on their vaccinations. See a vet if they get sick.

- **In the event of an epidemic or biological terrorism event, follow the advice of the authorities**. They may tell you to shelter in place. They may put you through a decontamination process. They may quarantine you.

- Listen to the media for information and instructions.

- Contact your local and state health departments for information.

With a little common sense and the proper precautions, you can avoid infectious diseases and keep from spreading them.

15. Chemical Events

The Basics

Chemicals are found everywhere. Many cannot be seen or smelled. Hazards can occur during production, storage, transportation, use, or disposal. Sources of these hazardous materials can be chemical manufacturers, service stations, hospitals, hazardous waste sites, and chemical carriers. Exposure can be unintentional (e.g., transportation accidents) or intentional (e.g., chemical terrorism). You and your community are at risk if a chemical is used unsafely or released in harmful amounts.

Chemical manufacturers are one source of hazardous materials, but there are many others, including service stations, hospitals, and hazardous materials waste sites.

Chemical warfare agents can be poisonous gasses, liquids, or solids. They are deployed in one or more of several ways: wet or dry aerosol, vaporization by heat, application to a specific site, and contamination of food, water, or medications.

The signs of a chemical attack or a chemical accident are:

- Dead plants, animals, insects
- Pungent odor
- Unusual clouds, vapors, droplets
- Discoloration of surfaces

Chemical contamination of the air might cause the following signs and symptoms in multiple patients:

- Tightness in the chest and difficulty breathing

- Nausea and vomiting
- Watery eyes or blurry vision
- Seizures

The Jargon

Blister agent—chemical warfare agents that cause blisters (e.g., mustard gas).

Blood agent—chemical warfare agents that deprive blood and organs of oxygen.

Choking agent—chemical warfare agents that attack the respiratory system, causing difficulty breathing (e.g., chlorine).

Cold, warm, and hot zones—Operational zones set up by teams responding to a hazardous materials incident. The Hot Zone is the area at the site of the release. The perimeter is determined by the substance, the size of the spill, and ambient conditions, often using a standard reference text called the *Emergency Response Guidebook* (U.S. Department of Transportation, ERG2004). Only trained personnel in specialized protective clothing may enter the Hot Zone. The Warm Zone is the area around the Hot Zone. It is used for decontamination, and usually requires specialized protective clothing. The Cold Zone surrounds the Warm Zone and is used for staging of responders and equipment, incident command, and medical support. It usually requires no protective clothing.

Confinement—Action taken to keep a material within a defined local area.

Corrosive—A liquid or solid that eats away another material.

Vehicles carrying hazardous materials are usually marked
with placards that identify the hazard.

Flash point—The lowest temperature at which a liquid will
give off enough flammable vapor to burn.

Insecticide—A chemical made to kill insects, usually
similar to nerve agents. Most can cause illness and death
in humans.

Metabolic agent—A chemical warfare agent that affects the
body's ability to use oxygen at the cell level (e.g., cyanide).

Nerve agent—Chemical warfare agents that affect the
nervous system. These are of great concern because of the
low amounts needed to cause death (e.g., sarin).

Protecting Yourself and Your Family

Before an Incident

- The Local Emergency Planning Committees (LEPCs) are responsible for collecting information about hazardous materials in the community and making this information available to the public upon request. The LEPCs also are responsible for developing an emergency plan to prepare for and respond to chemical emergencies in the community. The plan will include the ways the public will be notified and actions the public must take in the event of a release. Contact the LEPCs through your local emergency management office to find out more about chemical hazards and what needs to be done to minimize the risk to individuals and the community.

- Know the signs of a chemical incident.

During an Incident

Listen to local radio or TV for detailed information and instructions. Follow the instructions. Stay away from the area to minimize the risk of contamination. Some toxic chemicals are invisible and odorless.

- If you're told to evacuate, do so immediately. There may be very little time.
- If you're outside, stay uphill, upwind, upstream of the incident. Distance yourself at least a half a mile (8–10 blocks) from the hot zone.
- If you're in a vehicle, stop and take shelter in a building. If you can't risk leaving the vehicle, keep

the windows and vents closed and shut off the heater or air conditioner.

- If you're told to stay indoors, close and lock exterior doors and windows. Close vents, fireplace dampers, and as many interior doors as possible.

    - Turn off air conditioners and ventilation systems. In larger buildings, set the ventilation system to 100 percent recirculation (no outside air) or turn it off.

    - Go into your designated shelter room or an interior room with few or no exterior windows or doors. Take your disaster supplies kit with you.

    - Seal the doors, windows, and vents with plastic sheeting and duct tape. Stuff holes and cracks with material and seal with tape. (See chapter 8, "Evacuation and Shelter.")

- If the attack or exposure is indoors:

    - Get out quickly, covering your face with your shirt or other clean material.

    - Shed your clothes. Dry decontamination (shedding the clothes) removes up to 80 percent of the toxic agent.

    - Thoroughly rinse the skin. Flush irritated eyes for several minutes if possible.

    - Stay calm and follow instructions.

What about that expensive gas mask you bought for this very event? If you have a gas mask with appropriate filters or cartridges, and you remember how to put it on and check the seal, use it. Do NOT use the mask in low-oxygen atmospheres. For instance, if you're sheltering in place and you have sealed the room with plastic and duct tape, the oxygen level in the room will soon drop below the limit recommended by the mask manufacturer.

After a Hazardous Materials Incident

- Return home only when authorities say it is safe. Open windows and vents and turn on fans to provide ventilation.

- Act quickly if you have touched or been exposed to hazardous chemicals. Many chemicals are rapidly absorbed through the skin.

  - Follow decontamination instructions from local authorities. They might advise to take a thorough shower, or you may be told to follow another procedure. If you can't get instructions from an authority, follow the following general **dry decontamination procedures**:

    - Remove clothing, jewelry, eyeglasses, and other items in contact with the skin. Place exposed clothing and shoes in a plastic garbage bag and tie a knot in it, then place that in another plastic bag and tie it. Do not allow contaminated clothing to contact other people or objects. When authorities are available, ask them how to dispose of it. Dry decontamination will remove as much as 80 percent of the chemical.

  - **If wet decontamination** is recommended:

    - Use large amounts of soap and water.
    - If the eyes are affected, flush for 10–15 minutes.
    - Remove and discard contaminated contacts.

A Gas Mask Primer

You've heard a lot of talk about gas masks, but before you run out and buy one, it's important to know some basic information. A mask is no guarantee against the effects of a chemical or biological exposure. Only what's called Class A protective equipment (fully encapsulating protective suit with self-contained breathing apparatus, or SCBA) can provide total protection. Unless you plan to spend over a thousand dollars and carry this bulky equipment around with you, it's not something you should consider.

Gas masks come in several types. Half-masks cover the nose and mouth but not the eyes, and some chemical agents attack through or target the eyes. A full face masks covers the eyes, nose, and mouth. These can be effective if the seal is good. Half- and full-face filtered-air masks are called air purifying respirators (APR).

A PAPR, or positive pressure air-purifying respirator, pulls air through a filter and pumps it into the respirator, pressurizing it so leaks blow filtered air out rather than allowing contaminated air into the mask. Some APRs can be turned into PAPRs, but not all PAPRs can be used as APRs if the pump batteries run out.

Different filters provide different kinds of protection. Particulate filters filter out small airborne particles (e.g., fine particulate filters that are used against asbestos or biologic agents). Activated charcoal filters remove some chemical vapors and mists. Other chemicals can be removed by filters that neutralize chemical agents with a chemical reaction. Modern APR and PAPR filters use a combination of these methods. The filters are color-coded for specific groups of chemicals or particulate hazards according to NIOSH standards. Refer to the owner's manual for recommendations on which filters you will need to keep on hand.

If you don't have a gas mask, use a piece of cloth (bandana, T-shirt, etc.) or surgical mask snugly over nose and mouth. This will provide some protection against larger particulates and limited protection against vapors. It will not neutralize chemicals.

- ◆ Wash eyeglasses with soap and water.
- ◆ Dispose of clothes by double bagging in plastic garbage sacks. Don't touch the clothes. Use gloves and tongs and place them in the bag, too. Seal the bags.
- ◆ Ask the health department about disposal.
- ◆ Dress in clean clothes. If it was stored in a closet or drawers, it's probably safe.

- Seek medical care for unusual symptoms as soon as possible.
- Tell everyone who comes into contact with you that you may have been exposed.
- As soon as possible find out from local authorities how to clean up your land and property.
- Report any lingering vapors, unusual smells, or other hazards to your local law enforcement, fire department, or health department.

16. Nuclear & Radiological Emergencies

The Basics

A nuclear or radiological emergency is an event that poses a nuclear a radiological threat to public health and safety, property, or the environment.

Nuclear or radiological emergencies could include:

- An emergency at a nuclear facility, such as a nuclear power station.

- An emergency involving a nuclear-powered vessel.
- A transportation accident involving the shipment of radioactive material.
- An incident involving the loss, theft, or discovery of radioactive material.
- A terrorist attack utilizing radioactive materials, such as a "dirty bomb" or an RDD (radiological dispersion device using common explosives to spread radioactive material—this is NOT the same thing as a nuclear blast).
- A nuclear blast.

A nuclear blast is produced by a nuclear detonation. It involves the joining or splitting of atoms (called fusion and fission) to produce an intense pulse or wave of heat, light, air pressure, and radiation. It creates a large fireball, and everything inside of this fireball vaporizes and is carried upwards, creating a mushroom cloud. Radioactive material from the nuclear device mixes with the vaporized material in the mushroom cloud. It cools and condenses and forms particles. The condensed radioactive "dust" then falls back to the earth and is known as fallout. Radioactive fallout can be carried for many miles on wind currents and can contaminate anything on which it lands on. The effects on humans will depend on the size of the bomb and the distance the person is from the explosion. Injury or death may occur as a result of the blast itself, airborne debris, or burns. The intense light of the blast can cause serious eye damage. Victims near the blast site will be exposed to high levels of radiation and will develop radiation sickness (called acute radiation syndrome, or ARS). Burns will appear quickly but other signs and symptoms can take days to appear.

Two types of exposure from radioactive materials can occur from a nuclear blast: external exposure from the blast and fallout and internal exposure from contaminated air, food, and water. Exposure to very large doses of radiation may cause death within a few days or weeks. Exposure to lower doses may lead to cancer.

A nuclear power plant accident would not cause the same kind of destruction as a nuclear blast. Some radioactive material might be released in a plume, but no fallout is produced. The radiation hazard in the local area will depend on the type of accident, the amount of radiation released, and the weather. In case of an accident plant and local authorities would monitor the situation and issue instructions to the surrounding communities. If you hear news about an accident at a nearby nuclear plant, don't panic. Not all accidents will result in a release of radiation.

Every level of government responds in the event of a nuclear or radiological emergency. The response starts at the local level, and progresses to state and federal levels, depending upon the location, type, and size of the emergency.

The key to surviving a radiation emergency is to limit the amount of radiation you are exposed to. Use shielding, distance, and time.

- **Shielding:** A thick shield between yourself and the source will absorb some of the radiation.
- **Distance:** The farther away you are away from the source, the lower your exposure.
- **Time:** Less time near the source means less exposure.

The Jargon

Alpha and Beta particles—Forms of radiation that can be stopped by thin shielding (for Alpha) to moderate shielding (for Beta).

Blast shelter—A shelter that offers protection from blast pressure, radiation, heat, and fire.

Fallout shelter—Any protected space with an encasing structure thick and dense enough to block or absorb the radiation given off by fallout.

Gamma waves—A penetrating form of radiation that requires thick, dense shielding for protection.

Ionizing radiation—Radiation that can cause other atoms, including those in human tissue, to become charged.

Nuclear event—Nuclear detonation involving fusion and fission, leaving radioactivity and fallout behind.

Nuclear plant warnings—

> *Unusual Event:* A small problem with no expected radiation leak. No action necessary.
>
> *Alert:* A small problem with minor radiation leakage inside the plant. No action necessary.
>
> *Site Area Emergency:* Sirens may be sounded. Listen to media for information and instructions.
>
> *General Emergency:* Radiation leaks possible outside the plant and off the plant site. Listen to media for information and instructions. Follow instructions promptly.

Radiation—Electromagnetic energy released from a radioactive material.

Radioactive contamination—Deposition of radioactive material on surfaces.

Radioactive exposure—Penetration of the body by radiation. Exposed patients aren't necessarily contaminated (e.g., X-rays).

Radiological event—An event that may involve explosion and release of radioactivity but no fission or fusion.

RDD—Radiation dispersal device, or "dirty bomb."

Radiation units—*Roentgen* and the *rad* are measures of the effect radiation has on the absorbing material. The *rem* is a measure of biological damage to humans.

Protecting Yourself and Your Family

Prepare for these incidents the way you would prepare for other hazardous materials emergencies:

- Ask local authorities and plant officials about the hazards. Get specific information about the hazards to children and the chronically ill or pregnant. Ask where hazardous waste dumps are located and other questions you might have about transportation and storage of materials in your community. Attend public information meetings.
- Learn the community warning system and likely evacuation routes.
- Learn emergency plans for schools, daycares, nursing homes, and workplaces where your family members may be.
- Maintain a disaster supplies kit.
- Use your family communication plan.

Dirty Bomb or RDD

- If you are inside and there is an explosion inside or you are warned of a radiation release inside your building, cover your nose and mouth and go outside immediately. Find an undamaged building or other shelter and quickly get inside. Once inside, move to an interior room and close windows and doors. Turn off air conditioners, heaters, or other ventilation systems.

- If you are inside an undamaged building and there has been an explosion outside or authorities have warned of an outside release check, stay in the building. Move to an interior room. Close windows and doors, and turn off air conditioners, heaters or other ventilation systems.

- If you are outside and there is an explosion or authorities warn of a radiation release nearby, cover your nose and mouth and quickly go inside an undamaged building. If you think you have been exposed to radiation, take off your clothes, shower and wash your body with soap as soon as possible.

- Stay where you are, watch TV, listen to the radio, or check the Internet for official news as it becomes available.

Nuclear Blast

(recommendations from the World Health Organization)

If You Are Near the Blast When it Occurs

- Turn away and close and cover your eyes to prevent damage to your sight.
- Drop to the ground face down and place your hands under your body.
- Remain flat until the heat and two shock waves have passed.

If You Are Outside When the Blast Occurs

- Find something to cover your mouth and nose, such as a scarf, handkerchief, or other cloth.

- Remove any dust from your clothes by brushing, shaking, and wiping in a ventilated area—however, cover your mouth and nose while you do this.

- Move to a shelter, basement, or other underground area, preferably located away from the direction that the wind is blowing.

- Remove clothing since it may be contaminated. If possible, take a shower, wash your hair, and change clothes before you enter the shelter.

If You Are Already in a Shelter or Basement

- Cover your mouth and nose with a face mask or other material (such as a scarf or handkerchief) until the fallout cloud has passed.

- Shut off ventilation systems and seal doors or windows until the fallout cloud has passed. After the fallout cloud has passed, unseal the doors and windows to allow for some air circulation.

- Stay inside until authorities say it is safe to come out.

- Listen to the local radio or television for information and advice. Authorities may direct you to stay in your shelter or evacuate to a safer place away from the area.

- If you must go out, cover your mouth and nose with a damp towel.

- Use stored food and drinking water. Do not eat local fresh food or drink water from open water supplies.

- Clean and cover any open wounds on your body.

If You Are Advised to Evacuate

- Listen to the radio or television for information about evacuation routes, temporary shelters, and procedures to follow.

- Before you leave, close and lock windows and doors and turn off air conditioning, vents, fans, and furnace. Close fireplace and dampers.

- Take disaster supplies with you (such as a flashlight and extra batteries, battery-operated radio, first aid kit and manual, emergency food and water, non-electric can opener, essential medicines, cash, credit cards, and sturdy shoes).

A Radiation Detector Primer

This is another device that preparedness salesmen want to sell to you, but that most of us are not going to need or want. Aside from being expensive and bulky, chances are you're not going to have it with you when you need it.

The common detector is the Geiger counter. It has a tube that produces a clicking sound or a flash of light when alpha or beta particles enter it. The old bulky Cold War–era Geigers are still available . Some modern Geigers are available that plug into your laptop. A more sensible idea would be something like the RadDetect, a keychain-size device that has an alarm and flashing light that warn of high level radiation, a directional sensor, and a simple diagnostic feature that shows approximate roentgens per hour. It sells for under $150.

- Remember your neighbors may require special assistance, especially infants, elderly people, and people with disabilities.
- Evacuate to an emergency shelter immediately. Your children in school will be taken care of at school. Do not rush to get them.

Nuclear Power Plant Accident

- If you hear rumors of an accident, monitor local media for information and instructions.
- Unless instructed otherwise, bring family and pets inside and close and lock all doors and windows. Cover your mouth and nose while you're outside.
- Get in an interior room on a lower level and close and all doors and windows. Turn off air conditioning, fans, and furnace. Cover vents. Close fireplace dampers.
- Be prepared to evacuate immediately if told to do so by authorities. Remember neighbors with special needs.

When the Danger Has Passed

- Avoid using foods from the garden or milk from local animals until they are cleared by local authorities.
- Potassium Iodine, if taken soon enough after exposure, can block thyroid uptake of radioactive iodine and prevent thyroid cancer and other thyroid problems caused by inhaling or ingesting radioactive iodine. The decision to use and distribute potassium iodine to the community is up to the state. If you have potassium iodine in your kit, get the OK from

local health authorities or emergency management personnel before taking it.

17. Terrorism

The Basics

The specific tools of terrorism are covered in other sections of this chapter. Also, refer to the section on Civil Unrest.

Terrorism is the use of force or violence against persons or property for purposes of intimidation, coercion, or ransom. Terrorists often use threats to:

- Create fear among the public.
- Try to convince citizens that their government is powerless to prevent terrorism.
- Get immediate publicity for their causes.

Acts of terrorism include threats of attacks, assassinations, kidnappings, hijackings, bomb scares and bombings, cyber attacks (computer-based), and the use of chemical, biological, nuclear and radiological weapons.

High-risk targets for acts of terrorism include military and civilian government facilities, international airports, large cities, high-profile landmarks, large public gatherings, water and food supplies, utilities, corporate centers, and mail and mass transit systems.

During a terrorist attack you would need to rely on local police, fire, and other officials for instructions. Eventually state and federal agencies will become involved in the response.

The Jargon

CBRNE—The likely weapons of terrorism and mass destruction: chemical, biological, radiological, nuclear, and explosive; arson should be added.

Homeland Security Advisory—

Red (severe risk)—terrorist attack has occurred or is imminent.

Orange (high risk)—Attack likely, target not identified.

Yellow (elevated, significant risk)—Elevated risk, specific region or target not identified.

Blue (guarded, general risk)—No credible threats or specific targets.

Green (low risk)—Routine security advised.

Secondary device—A device set to detonate after police, fire, and emergency medical services are on the scene, or in safe areas where evacuees have gathered.

Terrorism—The use of violence or threats of violence to achieve a goal or to intimidate.

WMD—Weapon of mass destruction; any agent or weapon designed to cause mass casualties or massive infrastructure and property damage.

Protecting Yourself and Your Family

You can prepare in much the same way you would prepare for other crisis events.

The following are general guidelines recommended by FEMA:

- Be aware of your surroundings.

- Be aware of likely targets: skyscrapers and high rises, bridges and tunnels, pipelines, harbors, symbolic and religious landmarks, schools, government buildings, churches, malls, computer networks and data systems, power systems, vehicles of mass transit, and food and water supplies.

- Move or leave if you feel uncomfortable or if something does not seem right.

- Take precautions when traveling. Be aware of conspicuous or unusual behavior. Do not accept packages from strangers. Do not leave luggage unattended. You should promptly report unusual behavior, suspicious or unattended packages, and strange devices to the police or security personnel.

- Learn where emergency exits are located in buildings you frequent. Plan how to get out in the event of an emergency.

- Be prepared to do without services you normally depend on: electricity, telephone, natural gas, gasoline pumps, cash registers, ATMs, and Internet transactions.

- Work with building owners to ensure the following items are located on each floor of the building:

  - Portable, battery-operated radio and extra batteries.
  - Several flashlights and extra batteries.
  - First aid kit and manual.
  - Hard hats and dust masks.
  - Fluorescent tape to rope off dangerous areas.

When the threat level is Orange or Red:

- Report suspicious activities to 911 or your law enforcement services number.
- Expect delays, searches, and denial of access to public buildings.
- Expect traffic delays and restrictions.
- Avoid crowded areas or large crowds.
- Monitor media and be prepared to evacuate or shelter in place.
- Do not start or help circulate rumors.

18.   Civil Unrest & Armed Conflict

> *"Go to hell! It's every man for himself!"*
> —A New Orleans policeman to a stranded
> tourist in the chaos of Hurricane Katrina

The Basics

Civil unrest covers a big list of public disturbances by groups, often because of protest or outrage. It includes riots, strikes, uprising and rebellion, looting, sit-ins, demonstrations, parades, sabotage, kidnapping, shootouts and sniping, executions, bombings, and other forms of terrorism, street fighting, and civil war. In most places both the police and the military will be involved, often clashing violently with the dissident groups. Things can get particularly ugly because the motives are usually hate, resentment, and fear. Fortunately most civil unrest and armed conflict results from tensions that build up over a period of time, and we can sense when the time is right to leave for safer turf. Occasionally a single event results in a sudden rampage. The best way to avoid getting captured, injured, or killed in these situations is to avoid them entirely by getting out before they escalate or evacuating as soon as the opportunity presents itself. Once you're caught in the middle of it, getting out can be tough.

The Jargon

Boycott—A refusal by a group to use a service or product of a business or government as a form of protest or pressure.

Curfew—An order requiring the public or certain groups to get off and stay off the streets at a certain hour.

Looting—The criminal act of taking things from homes and buildings by forceful means.

Martial law—Temporary military rule imposed in an emergency.

Protest—A public gathering to express opposition.

Rebellion—An uprising meant to overthrow a government or ruling authority, or to oppose it by force.

Riot—A chaotic disturbance caused by a large number of people.

Strike—An event in which workers stop working in support or protest of decisions by their employers or government.

Protecting Yourself and Your Family

Before an Incident

- Make the basic preparations recommended in chapter 3. If you're in an exotic or foreign location your evacuation plan should include your likely evacuations destinations (e.g., the airport, the embassy, the closest border crossing, etc.) and some safe haven you can go to if you're unable to get to your evacuation destination. Include your family in the planning process so they know where to go. On your contact list include the phone numbers and locations of friendly embassies or consulates, police stations, hospitals, and airports. Keep a "hasty" pack of disaster supplies for each member of the family that they can grab at a moments notice. With your passports and other essential papers keep some emergency cash in the currency of the country you're in as well as the universal cash—the U.S. dollar. If you get cut off and stuck in the middle of the mess, money will be your key to safety. It doesn't hurt to have an emergency credit card, but I don't think rioters, terrorist, and crooked cops accept them.

- Stay informed and alert. There is usually some indication in the news that there are potential problems. There may be travel advisories issued from your embassy or the Department of State. Postpone or reroute your travel plans.

- Contact your embassy and let them know where you are. Give your itinerary to some friends who aren't traveling with you. *Authors note: I personally have had nothing but bad service from U.S. Embassies abroad. This has ranged from outright refusal to assist a large group of U.S. missionaries during South American riots and the ensuing violent revolution, to being scoffed at by embassy staff in the Republic of Georgia when the stairs to my hotel room in Kutaisi were rigged with a phone bomb, to being overruled by pencil-pushing embassy white-shirts in my field investigation of a suspicious death of an American advisor in the Middle East. I did learn some tricks when I was living in the Middle East: shmooz and brown-nose with the embassy staff and make friends there. Do the same with the international NGOs. You'll get access to all kinds of things, the most valuable of which might be information and protection when you need it the most.*

- Know the local laws and customs. Dress conservatively, and consider dressing like the locals.
- Be vigilant with personal and family security by:
  - Traveling in groups.
  - Keeping personal information secret.
  - Protecting your passport.
  - Being polite.
  - Keeping an emergency contact list with you.
  - Varying your routine so potential criminals or terrorists cannot predict your movements. Avoid walking slow and loitering or browsing.
  - Leaving when your gut tells you something bad is imminent.
- Be aware of current events and the local environment. The tension often builds over a period of days or weeks. When the tension is near the breaking point, there will be a palpable sense that something is about to happen. Your ability to tune into this will depend on your understanding of the culture, the routines, and the normal activity of the community you're in. Local residents will seem nervous. If asked, they might tell you what's going on. If locals warn you that the shit is about to hit the fan, get out.
- Travel with a small group of people for protection, but avoid other groups of people, especially large

groups. Do not go near demonstrations, meetings, or parades you don't know the meaning of. If there's palpable tension, avoid being in the street, even for parties or shopping in the open markets.

- Don't rubberneck. If something suspicious is happening, don't stop to see what's going on.

- Avoid mass transit and other forms of public transportation. Train stations and airports can get dangerously crowded when everyone is trying to get out at the same time. Your embassy might be able to suggest alternatives.

- If you're leaving a home or office behind, secure it. Looting is often the result of civil unrest. Lock doors and windows. Board them up from the inside and outside if possible. If there's time, take smaller valuables with you or stash them in a safe location.

- *Do not panic*. A calm demeanor will get you through some of the most tense confrontations.

- If rioting or street warfare breaks out while you're inside, stay there. Lock doors and windows and barricade them. Move to interior rooms to avoid bullets and rocks. Define two ways out for rapid escape in case of fire or inside attack. Call the embassy and the police.

- If you're outside and fighting is imminent or in progress, move away. Move slowly to avoid attention, and move diagonally with the flow of the crowd to eventually make your way to the side of the crowd. There are lots of things to think about. If you leave the crowd, will you be an easy target? If you stay with the crowd, will police and military mistake you for a participant? Some other recommendations:

    - Avoid major roads and public squares. Take the road less traveled.

A Body Armor Primer

I almost laughed when the county authorities insisted I wear body armor when I signed on to run an ambulance service in northeast Wyoming almost 20 years ago. It was a rough, Wild West environment to work in, and after the first couple of life-threatening incidents I wore the armor faithfully and felt vulnerable without it.

For most of us body armor is just another gadget the salesmen are trying to sell a paranoid public. There are those who actually do have reasons for concern, including wealthy business executives, government VIPs, body guards, security officers, law enforcement, and in some areas, fire and EMS personnel. Lately even teachers are starting to look at wearing body armor.

Body armor has changed over the decades to the point where now it's possible to get reasonable protection in a vest made from soft woven fibers. This "soft armor" is more tailored than traditional armor, making it easy to conceal and comfortable to wear.

Body armor's protection capability is rated I through IV, sometimes with an –A suffix that indicates soft armor. Class I armor will stop small caliber handgun bullets. Class IV can stop a close blast from a large-gauge shotgun.

As with any other gadget, don't bother buying it if you're not going to lug it around with you. The time you will need it will be the time you don't have it. For most of us, body armor will be a waste of money.

A Small Weapons Primer

I believe in the right to bear arms. It's a fundamental constitutional right. It's just too bad that some people can't control their weapons. From personal experience I can tell you that any handgun you keep in the home is more likely to be a weapon of homicide or suicide in your home and by family or friends than to be a weapon of self-defense against a criminal, a rioting crowd, or an intruder. Aside from the demise of two brothers and a nephew at the hands of their own weapons, my own experience on the street can't lie: In 17 years of paramedic practice I saw a few hundred suicides and homicides with personal weapons, but only a single incident where a weapon was used for personal protection. That should be a major deterrent to keeping guns in a family home, but in reality most people live under the delusion that something like that just can't happen to them.

A gun is another one of those gadgets the Chicken-Little salesmen want to sell us. If you decide to buy one, do it legally and get some training and a permit. Realize that pulling a weapon out during civil unrest implies you are committed to a violent act. Your actions will elicit one of two emotions: fear or anger. If your foes are afraid, you've probably won the battle. If your foes are pissed off, you may have made the worst mistake of your life.

If you decide you can't live without a firearm for personal protection, choose a handgun that is of sufficient caliber to neutralize a large adult. Experts pretty much agree that 9 mm is as small as you should go, and anything larger than a .38 Special or .357 Magnum is too big. Other considerations to make are price, your physical size, and hand strength. Revolvers are safer than semi-automatics, but semi-automatics are quicker to load and easier to conceal.

Once you've decided on a weapon, you'll need some training from experienced professionals who are street-smart. Plinking at cans isn't sufficient training for the close combat that typically occurs in armed urban unrest.

- ■ Avoid public transportation. It naturally draws crowds and can be a target. It can also be difficult to escape from.

- ■ If you're in a car, keep driving. Do not stop. Be suspicious of cars following you and cars slowing down in front of you. Do not stop if someone tries to wave you down. Go around crowds to avoid having to slow down.

- If you're caught in a rushing crowd, avoid getting crushed by moving away from points of escape and exits. Do whatever you can to avoid tripping or falling. Climb something to get above the crowd.

- Do NOT confront groups. Do not be insulting, combative, or defiant. And don't plead American citizenship. In today's world it's not a "Get Out of Jail Free" card, and it's likely to get you in deeper trouble.

- Be suspicious about police, military, and roadblocks. Act confident but not defiant. Ask for ID, but be polite.

- If you are confronted with an armed military, police, or paramilitary roadblock, stay calm. Cooperate but act confident, respectfully, and with a controlled degree of friendliness. The author's opinion is that it's better to act as though you are traveling to complete important but friendly business rather than letting on that you are fleeing and in panic mode. If you can convince them that they have a reason to let you go, you will be allowed to pass. If that ultimately means bribing them with money without implying that the bribe is immoral or unethical, so be it. If they're corrupt but not violently criminal, they'll take your money and let you pass.

Another experienced-based opinion from the author: I have found myself facing the muzzle of a police or military machine gun more often than I care to remember. In all cases the gunman has either been more scared than me, or a fearless bully with a grudge or agenda. In the first situation I felt like it was best to calm the gunman's fears and sympathize with the frightening job he has to do. In the second, I found that respect is what the gunman is looking for. Neither of these gunmen would be inclined to sympathize with a wailing idiot tearfully pleading for his own life. It's better to give them what they need and want, and maintain your demeanor.

19.   Explosives & Bombs

The Basics

An explosion is the sudden release of energy and the accompanying pressure (shock waves) exerted on surrounding materials by the expanding gas. An explosion can be the result of natural causes (volcanoes, for instance) or accidental or intentional causes such as hazardous materials accidents or terrorism. A bomb is a man-made explosive device. Destruction and injury are caused by the blast wave and the impact of fragments propelled by the blast.

The most common explosion injuries are penetrating and blunt trauma. Death is often caused by lung injuries ("blast lung"). Burns are also common. Explosions in confined spaces (buildings, mines, vehicles) and structural collapse will increase the injuries and damage.

The Jargon

Detonator—A device used to set off an explosive charge.

Explosives—A Prepared chemical that produces a rapid, violent chemical change on being heated or impacted.

High explosives—An explosive that produces gas and pressure at a very high rate.

IED—Improvised explosive device (including "pipe bombs").

Propellants—An explosive used to propel projectiles.

How to Protect Yourself and Your Family

Preparing for a Building Explosion

Explosions can collapse buildings and cause fires. People who live or work in a multi-level building can do the following:

- Know emergency evacuation procedures. Know where emergency exits are located.
- Keep fire extinguishers in working order. Know where they are located and learn how to use them.
- Learn first aid.
- Building owners should keep a disaster supplies kit on each floor of the building. It should contain the following items:
  - The basic items listed in chapter 2
  - Several additional flashlights and extra batteries
  - First aid kit
  - Several hard hats
  - Fluorescent tape to rope off dangerous areas

Bomb Threats

If you receive a bomb threat, get as much information from the caller as possible. Keep the caller on the line and record everything that is said. Then notify the police and the building management.

If you are notified of a bomb threat, do not touch any suspicious mail or packages. Clear the area around suspicious mail, packages, or unidentified unattended bags or boxes and notify the police immediately. While evacuating the building, don't stand in front of windows, glass doors, or other potentially hazardous areas. Do not block doorways, sidewalks, or streets to be used by emergency officials or others still exiting the building.

Suspicious Parcels and Letters

Be wary of suspicious packages and letters. They can contain explosives, chemical, or biological agents. Be suspicious of mail and packages that:

- Are unexpected or from someone unfamiliar to you.
- Have no return address, or have one that can't be verified as legitimate.
- Are marked with restrictive endorsements, such as "Personal," "Confidential," or "Do not x-ray."
- Have protruding wires or aluminum foil, strange odors, or stains.
- Show a city or state in the postmark that doesn't match the return address.
- Are of unusual weight, given their size, or are lopsided or oddly shaped.
- Are marked with any threatening language.
- Have inappropriate or unusual labeling.
- Have excessive postage or excessive packaging material such as masking tape and string.
- Have misspellings of common words.
- Are addressed to someone no longer with your organization or are otherwise outdated.
- Have incorrect titles or title without a name.

- Are not addressed to a specific person.
- Have handwritten or poorly typed addresses.

With suspicious envelopes and packages other than those that might contain explosives, take these additional steps against possible biological and chemical agents:

- Refrain from eating or drinking in a designated mail handling area.
- Place suspicious envelopes or packages in a plastic bag or some other type of container to prevent leakage of contents. Never sniff or smell suspect mail.
- If you do not have a container, then cover the envelope or package with anything available (e.g., clothing, paper, trash can) and do not remove the cover.
- Leave the room and close the door, or section off the area to prevent others from entering.
- Wash your hands with soap and water to prevent spreading any powder to your face.
- If you are at work, report the incident to your building security official or an available supervisor, who should notify police and other authorities without delay.
- List all people who were in the room or area when this suspicious letter or package was recognized. Give a copy of this list to both the local public health authorities and law enforcement officials for follow-up investigations and advice.
- If you are at home, report the incident to local police.
- Leave the building as quickly as possible. Do not stop to retrieve personal possessions or make phone calls.

- If things are falling around you, get under a sturdy table or desk until they stop falling. Then leave quickly, watching for weakened floors and stairs and falling debris as you exit.

- Keep in mind that a second device or threat may be planted by the bomber. When you get out of the building, move away from the area. Do not stand in the open to watch the activity.

If There Is a Fire

- Stay low to the floor and exit the building as quickly as possible.

- Cover your nose and mouth with a wet cloth.

- When approaching a closed door, use the back of your hand to feel the lower, middle, and upper parts of the door. Never use the palm of your hand or fingers to test for heat: burning those areas could impair your ability to escape a fire (i.e., ladders and crawling).

- If the door is NOT hot, open slowly and ensure fire and/or smoke is not blocking your escape route. If your escape route is blocked, shut the door immediately and use an alternate escape route, such as a window. If clear, leave immediately through the door. Be prepared to crawl. Smoke and heat rise. The air is clearer and cooler near the floor.

- If the door is hot, do not open it. Escape through a window. If you cannot escape, hang a white or light-colored sheet outside the window, alerting firefighters to your presence.

- Heavy smoke and poisonous gases collect first along the ceiling. Stay below the smoke at all times.

- Do not light a match.

- Do not move about or kick up dust. Cover your mouth with a handkerchief or clothing.
- Rhythmically tap on a pipe or wall so that rescuers can hear where you are. Use a whistle if one is available. Shout only as a last resort when you hear sounds and think someone will hear you—shouting can cause a person to inhale dangerous amounts of dust.

20. Threats From Space

We all know from watching *Armageddon* over and over again on the cable channels that when the big asteroid comes to get us, we'll send up a band of renegade oil drillers to blow it up with giant nuclear bombs. I feel so safe now.

In actuality, we do have at least two worries from space: comets and asteroids. Comets are immense collections of dust, ice, and gas. Theoretically a comet could sneak up on us before we saw it and leave us less than a year to figure out what to do with it. In our neck of the cosmic woods comets are rare. We're about a hundred times more likely to get smacked with an asteroid.

Asteroids are largely composed of stone and iron. We can see them coming because they're more dense. The problem is that there are millions of them in the asteroid belt between Mars and Jupiter, and sometimes they come close to earth. We've been hit before. Sooner or later we'll be hit again.

An asteroid spotted in 2004 is a good example. Scientists and computers predict that in 2029 it will come as close as 15,000 miles from earth. That is a long way out from our perspective, but in astronomical terms it's very close. Some scientists think it will get close again a few years later, possibly much closer. If it were to hit us, say in an ocean, it would cause the tsunami from hell, drowning millions and destroying farmlands a hundred or so miles inland, resulting in crop failure, famine, and disease. If it hit land, the impact would pulverize an area the size of Utah and Nevada combined and send a dust cloud into the atmosphere that would cause serious global cooling, crop failure, and resulting famine and disease.

Our plan is simple. If the evil asteroid heads in our direction, we'll send up a spacecraft to tow it off course. We can be assured that Bruce Willis will not be on the tugboat.

Before the Collision

Let's go back to the scenario. We've spotted the doomsday asteroid heading our way. We've got a few years to get ready. If we're seriously worried about it, we build a two year disaster supplies kit. We pack a lot of thick books, because with our neighbors all dead and civilization in total collapse, it's going to be a long two years. Oh, guys, pack some Viagra, because you'll be busy trying to repopulate the planet.

During the Collision Event

If you're lucky enough to be on the other side of the planet when it hits, your short-term survival is relatively secure. If not, kiss your ass good-bye.

Chapter 11
Public Health in Disasters

There are two distinct parts to public health in terms of disasters and emergencies. The first has to do with what various levels of government public health agencies do to prepare and respond to disasters. The second is the public's role in maintaining its health and minimizing the effects of disasters.

1.   The Government

The initial responsibility for responding to an emergency and protecting the people, property, and environment within its jurisdiction falls to the local government. In public health matters this is the local health department. Until 9/11 the local health departments were largely left out of the local and state emergency planning processes. As the country began to focus on terrorism and emerging infections as major threats to the nation, funding from the CDC and HHS was directed to the state departments of health and much of that trickled down to the locals. Along with the money came pressure from the Feds for health departments to coordinate more closely with local and state emergency services and emergency management offices to develop coordinated plans and resources, and to coordinate in incident management. Public Health from the local HDs (health departments) right up the top federal health offices were slow to catch up and reluctant to take advice from "a bunch of dumb cops and firemen," as one of my health department colleagues put it. Immediate response as seen through the eyes of first responders like fire, police and EMS did not seem to mix well with the typical health department attitude of "wait and see what develops." But in the last five years some enormous changes have happened. Health departments have become disaster response experts in their own right, and have become an integral part of the primary disaster response team if not the first response team.

State and local health departments develop preparedness plans for mass dispensing of medication and vaccinations, protocols for quarantine and isolation, conduct disease surveillance and epidemiologic investigations, develop emergency communications and public information systems, coordinate laboratory testing and reporting, conduct professional workforce training and public awareness education, advise other responders and emergency managers on public health matters, and facilitate and take part in exercises and drills. Most states maintain a Web-based information exchange system to supplement the Health Alert Network and provide an independent source of regional health alert and response information. In many cases the health department is an integral part of the local hazardous materials response team. State and local HDs work closely with other professional and volunteer organizations like the Red Cross and the Medical Reserve Corps to provide services and resources.

The principle federal public health agency is the Department of Health and Human Services (HHS). The goal of HHS is to ensure sustained public health preparedness in defense against terrorism, infectious disease outbreaks, medical emergencies, and other public health threats. To do it, HHS works to:

- Monitor, assess, and follow up on public health
- Ensure the safety of responders
- Ensure the food supply is safe
- Provide medical, public health, and mental/behavioral advice
- Establish and maintain a record of exposures or contaminations by a given agent

HHS works closely with state, local, and tribal public health, the Department of Homeland Security, and other agencies and partners to provide public health and medical services advice. HHS has the authority to declare a public health emergency and to conduct and support research and investigation into the cause, treatment, and prevention of a disease or disorder. It also has the authority to make and enforce regulations including isolation and quarantine, to prevent introduction, transmission, and spread of diseases into the U.S. or between states.

There are several federal programs that help local and state health authorities forecast and manage emergencies.

- *Detecting disease threats.* Programs include syndromic surveillance, or monitoring and analysis of disease patterns; BioSense, which monitors hospital data and flags possible health emergencies, and an air monitoring system called Biowatch; in place in 30 cities.
- *Responding to disease threats.* This includes biological and chemical response labs under the Lab Response Network (LRN). The Health Alert Network (HAN) is a nationwide integrated electronic information and communications system for distributing health alerts, prevention guidelines, surveillance information, and

lab data. The Epidemic Information Exchange passes epidemiological information via the Web-based Epi-X Network. Finally, the CDC may deploy a rapid response team to the affected state.

- *Containment of disease threats.* The Centers for Disease Control (CDC) maintains a Strategic National Stockpile. The SNS is a national cache of strategically placed critical medical supplies to supplement state and local public health agencies in the event of a national emergency. SNS is designed to deploy within 12 hours of the decision to do so. To deploy the SNS, a governor must request assistance from HHS or CDC. HHS determines what action will be taken. Once the SNS is deployed, local agencies distribute the supplies. Other programs include vaccination, isolation and quarantine protocols, and the National Disaster Medical System. The NDMS provides medical services to local and state agencies during major emergencies to support local hospital systems. NDMS teams are deployed when state or local governments request it, or in case of a national emergency. NDMS teams include the Disaster Medical Assistance Teams (DMAT), Disaster Mortuary Operational Response Team (DMORT, Veterinary Medical Assistance Team (VMAT), National Nursing Response Team (NNRT), and the National Pharmacist Response Team (NPRT). In addition, the Federal government maintains the commissioned corps of the U.S. Public Health Service and the Medical Reserve Corps, an organization composed of local volunteer medical and public health professionals.

The Red Cross is a nonprofit volunteer organization. It is mentioned here because in 1905 it was given authority through a congressional charter to provide assistance in disasters. The ARC works closely with federal, state, and local governments to provide emergency first aid, health care in shelters, supportive counseling, augmentation of medical and health staff to bolster surge capacity, assistance with meeting basic needs, and the provision of blood products.

2.   The Public

People affected by disasters are more likely to become ill and to die from diseases related to inadequate sanitation and water supplies than from any other single cause. The most important of these are the diarrheal diseases and others transmitted by the fecal-oral route that are encouraged by inadequate sanitation, poor hygiene practice, and contaminated or insufficient water supplies.

Sanitation refers to the collection and disposal of human excreta, domestic and institutional solid waste, and dead bodies. Despite its close link to the very common causes of serious disease and death, emergency sanitation is often neglected. Volunteers do not perceive cleaning up other people's wastes as exciting—it's easier to focus on rescuing the trapped, feeding the starving, and treating the injured. For local government agencies the problem is enormous; faced with a large population with no functioning sanitation system, where do you start?

In these circumstances it is absolutely critical that you do your part to maintain public health. It is your moral responsibility to practice basic hygiene during the emergency period.

- Always wash your hands with soap and water that has been boiled or disinfected:
  - Before preparing or eating food
  - After using the toilet
  - After cleanup activities
  - After handling articles contaminated with bad water or sewage
  - After first aid activities, and between each patient
- As much as possible use disposable paper or plastic plates, cups, and utensils.
- If you're sheltering with a group, take the initiative and insist on changes if the food preparation and kitchen hygiene are sub-standard. Better yet, volunteer to help. Insist that your companions and shelter-mates maintain proper personal hygiene. If sanitation issues arise, volunteer to help.
- If you are sick, seek medical attention and then isolate yourself and your personal items as much as reasonably possible. Consider wearing a face mask to protect others from becoming infected.
- Follow the advice of the authorities. Most of them are politicians. Politicians understand that if they screw up, they lose votes. Of course they can and will make mistakes, but they're going to try to do the most good for the greatest number of people, because that's how elections are won, and their subordinates know that that's how they keep their jobs.

Chapter 12
Business

Here are some harsh statistics: The American economy relies on small businesses, and 25 percent of small businesses do not reopen after they are directly impacted by a major disaster. The indirect impacts can shut you down, too: After the 9/11 attacks, tourist businesses 4,000 miles away on the island of Maui bit the dust.

Most big corporations are likely to have their own risk management team and an emergency planner on staff. Small business owners don't have that luxury. Use the references in the back of the chapter to seek out an appropriate template for business disaster plans that will ensure **continuity of operations** (COOP). Here's an outline of the essential steps you'll be taking:

1. *Do some disaster intelligence work.* Get to know what hazards can affect your area. Talk to other business owners in your area about their own plans. Get some information from the FEMA and Red Cross Web sites, or any of the other sites noted in this chapter.

2. *Do some structural mitigation.*

   - Bolt towering bookcases and stock cases to wall studs.

   - Protect fragile objects by securing them to a stand or shelf.

   - Move large and heavy objects to lower shelves.

   - Install drawer and cabinet latches to keep them from flying out and dumping.

- Use eye-screws to securely fasten frames and mirrors to the walls.

- Secure the hot water heater to the wall using plumber's tape or strap iron.

- Consider hiring a professional to install flexible connector to gas appliances and equipment, window shutters, and automatic fire sprinklers.

3. As your plan evolves your major concerns are going to be human resources, physical resources, and business continuity. How would a disaster affect you, your staff, your customers, and your workplace? How will you continue to serve your customers? Involve your employees and customers in the planning process.

4. *Develop your plan.*

- Maintain and carry with you a contact list (numbers and addresses) of key employees and customers.

- On your office voice mail system, designate a remote number on which you can leave recorded messages. Give the number to all your employees.

- Consider getting programmable call forwarding for your main business lines so you can reprogram them to ring elsewhere when necessary.

- Consider leaving a key and alarm codes with building security or a trusted friend or employee who lives closer than you to the office.

- Install emergency lights that turn on when the power goes out.

- Back up computer data throughout the day (see chapter 10). Keep a backup off site.

- Use UL-listed surge protectors and battery backup systems (UPS).

- Get a NOAA Weather Radio with a tone alert. Keep it turned on and listen when it alerts.

- Stock the minimum supply of office goods and equipment and disaster supplies that you would need to continue business in austere conditions.

- Familiarize yourself with your business insurance policy and modify to cover the hazards in your area. Include special riders for expensive equipment and consider purchasing business continuity or business interruption insurance to cove the loss of profits.

- Formulate a contingency plan to maintain operations if the company's location is destroyed.

- Keep a disaster supplies kit at the office (see Chapter 2), with enough food, water, and other basic items to take care of your staff and customers for an unexpected day or two of confinement.

5. *Get your employees and customers involved.* Designate a security and safety officer for each shift. Make sure that person has all the contact numbers and access information he/she needs. Explain your disaster plan to the staff and train using the plan.

Web sites with essential information:

- *www.ready.gov*—for risk analysis and disaster planning materials
- *www.ibhs.org*—for information on specific hazards
- *www.dconline.org*—to connect with contractors
- *www.sba.gov/disaster/getready.html*—for planning tips

Chapter 13
Special Needs Populations

Special needs populations are those not sufficiently addressed by local or family disaster plans. These are people who cannot independently access and use the resources in our plans and for whom preparedness and recovery will be more difficult. They include those who are mentally or physically disabled, those with limited English skills, people who live in austere remote locations, those who are culturally isolated, medically or chemically dependent, homeless, frail or elderly, children, and the impoverished. There's a long list of groups that could qualify as having special needs, and this chapter could be an inch thick before we covered half of them. We'll limit the specifics to a handful of groups, and the information should apply in general to other groups.

Another special need population is the pets that comfort us and the animals that feed us, who depend on us for their safety and well-being.

1.   Humans

Infants and Children

Make sure your disaster suplies kit includes enough formula, baby food, bottles, diapers, toys, and games to keep the child well fed and comfortable.

Parents and guardians should be familiar with emergency procedures at the schools and day cares their children attend. Their emergency information on file at the school should be up to date. This information should include permission and contact information for someone who can pick up your child from the school if you are unable to.

Make arrangements for latch-key kids in case of emergencies. Designate a caretaker and a safe haven for them to be at when you're not available during an emergency. Don't forget to tell the child and the caretaker about it.

Feeble, Disabled, or Chronically Ill Persons

Those needing medications. Keep at least a week supply in the disaster supply kit. Refresh the medications by rotating them. Keep a note of the name and dosage in case EMS or others need to assist the patient in taking the meds. If you have medical alert tags, wear them.

Those needing mechanical or electronic adjuncts.

- Persons confined to a wheelchair should store essential emergency supplies and medications in a bag to be kept under the chair or on the back of the wheelchair. If the wheelchair is electric, keep extra batteries and a charger on hand.

- Life support equipment such as oxygen tanks should be securely fashioned so they don't roll away or fall over. Keep an emergency generator or an adequate inverter or USP on hand to provide backup electricity for electronic life support equipment.

- Replace or rotate hearing aid batteries frequently. Have access to writing materials to help communicate. Ask someone to be responsible for passing on all the important disaster information to the deaf person.

2.   Animals

Pets

Keep your animal up to date on vaccinations and make sure they are wearing vaccination and identification tags. If you plan to evacuate, write your contact information on a piece of tape and secure it to the animal's collar.

Include enough dry food and water in your disaster supplies kit to last the same length of time your own food and water last.

Bring your animals inside during the emergency. Pets can sense the tension in a disaster situation and they may be aggressive or try to run away. Lost pets will have a hard time finding their way back if the disaster has altered the environment. Keep pets confined or tied up for their own protection. Use a leash to walk them or when you take them out for potty breaks.

Evacuate your pets with you, but if you must leave your pet behind or can't find it, leave some dry food out for it and some water in a container that won't tip over.

In your disaster kit you'll want to keep food and water for the pet, copies of the vaccination records, a current photo of your pets, a week's supply of pet medications, if any, cat litter and a litter box, and a portable kennel (travel box).

Include your pets in your disaster plan. Your plan should include a safe place to take your pet. Most community emergency shelters will not take animals because of health and safety considerations. If you know a disaster is approaching, call ahead to confirm your pet's arrangements.

If you have small pets, including rodents, reptiles, or birds, plan ahead of an event what you will need to provide the basic needs of that animal while sheltering or on the road. Do they need heating pads, cages or carriers, water bottles, special food?

Farm Animals

Develop a farm safety and evacuation plan, and make sure your family and farmhands know the plan and where to find it. Include your neighbors and be familiar with your neighbor's animals and plans.

Before an event:

- Make a firebreak around all buildings.
- Clear weeds and trim trees close to buildings.
- Clean roofs and gutters.
- Repair exposed wires, structural supports, and waterways.
- Clearly label utility and equipment shutoffs.
- Store hay, gasoline, and other combustibles or flammables away from animal barns.
- Remove overhanging trees that could fall on buildings or animals.
- Maintain adequate water supplies and sources.

During a disaster follow the recommendations given in the other chapters.

Nervous farm animals can be dangerous. Remember that your own safety is your primary concern. If you can do so without endangering yourself, lead your animals to safety from structural threats, rising water, and other hazards.

Give water freely to animals. They can go long periods without food, but only a day or two without water. Identify sources of feed and water prior to an event. Feed the animals adequately. Herbivores need about 1 to 2 percent of their body weight in the form of roughage daily.

If you must leave your animals behind, hang a highly visible sign on a window or door saying the breed and number of animals you're leaving behind. Put extra food and water close to the animals. Don't tie them or confine them in an area that could be destroyed. Pasture them if possible.

Report lost or found animals to emergency authorities.

Chapter 14
Dealing with It Where You Are

We've thoroughly discussed what to do at home, work, and while driving. We talked about integrating school and work plans with your own. Now let's look at some unique situations that we haven't covered.

1. Airplane Crashes

Given the nature of mass transportation systems, we are largely at the mercy of transportation and homeland security authorities to keep us informed and safe. With the size and carrying capacity of airplanes increasing (the Airbus A380 carries 800), we can expect airplane tragedies to be more catastrophic.

So . . . let's say you've done your homework and checked all the travel advisories and the world seems to be at peace on the day you board your next flight. Your flight leaves on schedule, on takeoff things go to hell in a hand basket, and the plane crashes. How could you have increased your odds of survival?

In an airplane crash that is actually survivable, which is pretty much limited to crashes on takeoff and landing, your survival depends upon how long it takes you to get unbuckled, find a way out, and get out before the flames and smoke kill you. A few seconds either way will make the difference between life and death.

Here's what you can do to increase your odds:

- The most dangerous parts of a flight are the takeoff and landing. Take a nonstop flight to reduce the number of times you take off or land.

- The idea that a seat in the tail or over the wing is safer than another seat is nonsense. The safest seat will be the one closest to the exit.

- Listen carefully to the safety briefing at the start of the flight. See and recognize the exits. Read the safety briefing card stashed in the seat pocket in front of you. Learn the configuration of the aircraft.

- Count the rows between your seat and the closest exits.

- If the plane crashes, unbuckle as fast as possible and move to the assigned or closest exit. If that exit is blocked, head for another.

- In the darkness and smoke, keep low, but do not lose your balance and fall. You will be trampled.

2.   Shipwrecks

Going on a cruise? Go with a reputable company with a good safety record. If they're complying with national and international standards, emergency information will be readily available and safety equipment will be adequate.

The captain of a passenger ship will periodically hold fire and lifeboat drills. They are intended to give the crew practice and show the passengers how to act in the event of an emergency. Passengers should participate.

Notices are usually posted in plain view in each passenger cabin or stateroom. The notice explains:

- How to recognize the ship's emergency signals.
- The location of life preservers.

- How to put on the life preserver, and the passenger's lifeboat assignment.

Passenger ships carry a variety of survival craft. Passengers are assigned to lifeboats. The total capacity of all the survival craft on board will exceed the total number of passengers and crew.

When an accident happens, crew members are generally responsible for assisting and directing passengers.

- Direction signs showing how to reach lifeboats are usually posted in passageways and stairways throughout the ship.
- The crewmember in charge of each lifeboat will muster the passengers assigned to that lifeboat, and give passengers any final instructions necessary in the proper method of donning and adjusting their life preservers.
- If there is any portion of the emergency procedures the passenger doesn't understand, they should question the crew until the instructions are clearly understood.
- In the water, row or swim away from a sinking ship to avoid being pulled by the undertow.
- Huddle together for additional warmth. To minimize the loss of body heat, float quietly and avoid swimming.

3.   High-Rises & Skyscrapers

A high-rise is commonly any building over four stories high. People trapped in a burning high-rise building will jump to their deaths or try to climb down anything they can hang out the window . . . whatever they can do to keep the fire and smoke from killing them. When buildings are constructed beyond the reach of a fire department's highest ladder, important firefighting strategies are removed from their inventory.

It's impossible for hundreds or thousands of people to evacuate a burning building quickly. We have seen some very grim reminders of that in the last couple of decades. Firefighters are forced to try to extinguish the fire while most of the occupants remain inside. Even so, the crowds will attempt to evacuate, communication with everyone will be impossible, and chaos will result.

The options are rather limited in a sudden disaster directly affecting a high-rise building.

Before an Event

- Make sure the alarms and sprinklers are working and know what they sound like.
- Know the evacuation routes that are posted on your floor walls.

During an Event

- Stay calm.
- If you detect a fire, activate the alarm and get out.
- Avoid taking elevators, which can stop and trap you between floors.
- Listen to the advice of local government officials and follow the building or business disaster plan.
- If you're told to shelter in place, go to an interior room on the same floor you're on, and shelter there.

- If told to evacuate, follow the advice of local officials and the commands of building security or management staff.
- If your exit route is blocked by smoke:
  - Crawl low to the floor.
  - In a room, close all doors between you and the smoke and seal the cracks around doors and vents. If possible, open exterior windows slightly at the top and bottom to provide some limited ventilation.
  - At the window, signal to rescuers. Call the fire department and give them your location.

Extreme Survival Gear

So you've been thinking about paying all kinds of money for an external personal or group high-rise escape system. Be careful you don't confuse what's real with deluded fantasy and your unfulfilled need to be Spiderman or Superwoman. External systems basically fall into five categories:

1. Slides and chutes
2. Rappelling and lowering systems
3. External elevator pods or platforms
4. Parachutes
5. Ziplines

The major problems with these systems is their inherent exposure to the sources of structural damage: flame and heat so intense that it vaporizes nylon, toxic atmospheres that asphyxiate the user, glass and metal shards that will slice right through tensioned rope systems. Over two-thirds of high-rise fires start on the fourth floor or below, which means if you're above the fourth floor, all that heat and smoke is headed your way. A second but important problem is the hazards these devices pose because of a lack of training. The third problem, of course, is that they're gravity-powered, and when something goes wrong the results will probably be fatal.

Probably the most interesting of these external escape devices are the skyscraper escape parachutes. Jumping from a high-rise is dangerous even for experienced BASE jumpers. The danger is amplified by inexperience, flying debris, and intense heat. The heat can produce winds that can easily push a jumper into the wall. Many escape chutes are designed for light loads and quick descents. Anything that will drop you more than 20 feet per second is likely to cause serious injury or death.

If you're determined to have a self-rescue system, the easiest, smallest, most inexpensive is probably a basic rappel system. This consists of a harness, a rappel device, and a rope long enough to reach the bottom, stored in a rope bag for easy deployment. Get some coaching on rope construction, rappel devices, anchoring, and rappelling from a real expert (a well respected caver, climber, or canyoneer).

4.   The Subway or Metro

Disasters in the world's subways and transit trains are not uncommon. Fires have been the traditional problem, but in recent years bombs and chemical attacks have stolen our attention. The 2003 train car fire in South Korea and the sarin gas attack in the Tokyo subway in 1995 are the most frequently cited examples. The former killed almost 200

	Likelihood of hardware or soft goods failure due to damage	Likelihood of operator error without monthly hands-on training	Bulk	Persons	Cost
Slides and chutes	Moderate	Moderate	Moderate	All in rapid succession	Moderate
Single line rappelling and lowering systems	High	High for rappel systems, moderate for lowering systems	Low	Lowers—all in slow succession; Rappels—anyone with a compatible harness and rappel device, in slow succession	Low
External elevator pods or platforms	Moderate	High	High, but usually stored externally	Groups of 8–30, in slow succession	High
Parachutes	Low	High	Low	One at a time, and only those who have them	Moderate
Ziplines	Moderate to high	Moderate to high	Low	One at a time, limited to equipment on hand	Low to moderate

Comparative features of high-rise evacuation systems

people, the latter killed a dozen. The 1995 subway train fire in Baku, Azerbaijan, got far less attention than the Sarin attack, but is an even more frightening example of the destruction that can occur in an underground incident. Over 300 died in Baku. From these and other disasters we can deduce some common-sense precautions:

- Use underground transit systems when they are less crowded. Not only are crowds a target, but in confined areas like a subway system, panicked crowds can trample anyone in the way and block exits, gates, stairs, and turnstiles.

- Being able to exit from the train car, the platform, and the station can be the key to survival. Sit close to the car exit. Familiarize yourself with the configuration of the platforms and memorize all the exits at the stations you frequent.

- Be alert and aware of your location relative to stations and exits. In case there's an incident between stations, you may need to know which is closest.

- Know the location of emergency intercoms and telephones in the cars and on the platforms. Report emergencies and suspicious activities and packages to the train operator or the station manager via these intercoms, directly to nearby police, or by phone to the common emergency number (911 in the U.S.).

- Know the locations of doors, overhead escape hatches, and fire extinguishers. You'll be able to get most of this information from maps and notices on the walls of the car, but some of it might require a little more investigation.

- In the event of an incident, stay calm and make as little noise as possible so you can hear instructions over the speaker systems.

- Stay in the train car unless told by authorities or forced by conditions to exit.
- The tracks are dangerous. Avoid exiting onto the tracks. In addition to passing traffic, there's the danger of coming in contact with powerful electrical currents (e.g., the third rail that supplies power to the train).

In dense metropolitan areas where the masses depend on the subway to get around, an incident that shuts down the subway generates a transportation mess for thousands. To alleviate potential problems, learn alternate ways of getting where you need to go (bus lines, taxis, the shortest walking route).

Refer to the section on chemical events for information on hazardous materials such as those that would be encountered in a gas attack by terrorists. If there is a chemical release in your vicinity you will probably notice large numbers of people coughing, rubbing their eyes, vomiting, or having difficulty breathing. To protect yourself, you need to shield yourself from contact with the chemical and get some distance between you and the "hot zone." Cover your nose, mouth, and as much of your face and skin as possible as quickly as possible, and try to exit the area. Seek advice and medical assistance from emergency responders.

If you're a regular commuter on an underground system, you might consider adding a few items to your basic go-kit (see the Appendix 7, "Go–Kits"). Add a small LED headlamp, extra batteries, and a multi-tool. An N95 mask is inexpensive and can provide some respiratory protection from particulates and chemical droplets. An emergency poncho or light rain-shell jacket takes up almost no room in your kit and can provide some protection from contamination.

In the case of a fire, the immediate life-threatening problem will be smoke—carbon monoxide and other fire gases. A quality escape hood ("smoke hood") could provide several minutes of breathable air, but is bulkier than most people are willing to carry on a daily basis. Air Purifying Respirators (APRs and PAPRs) are even bulkier and are likely to be left at home. In addition, none of these devices will protect you from an oxygen-depleted atmosphere.

5.   In a Foreign Land

The following information is quoted from the U.S. State Department's *www.travel.state.gov* Web site:

"Earthquakes, hurricanes, political upheavals, acts of terrorism, and hijackings are only some of the events threatening the safety of Americans abroad. Each event is unique and poses its own special difficulties. However, for the State Department there are certain responsibilities and actions that apply in every disaster or crisis.

When a crisis occurs, the State Department sets up a task force or working group to bring together in one set of rooms, all the people necessary to work on that event. Usually this Washington task force will be in touch by telephone 24 hours a day with our Ambassador and Foreign Service Officers at the embassy in the country affected.

Within a task force, the immediate job of the State Department's Bureau of Consular Affairs is to respond to the thousands of concerned relatives and friends who begin to telephone the State Department immediately after the news of a disaster is broadcast.

Relatives want information on the welfare of their family members and on the disaster. The State Department relies on its embassies and consulates abroad for hard information. Often these installations are also affected by the disaster and lack electricity, phone lines, gasoline, Nevertheless, foreign service officers work hard to get information back to Washington as quickly as possible. This is rarely as quickly as the press is able to relay information. Foreign Service Officers cannot speculate; their information must be accurate. Often this means getting important information from the local government, which may or may not be immediately responsive.

Welfare and Whereabouts

As concerned relatives call in, officers of the Bureau of Consular Affairs collect the names of the Americans possibly involved in the disaster and pass them to the embassy and consulates. Officers at post attempt to locate these Americans in order to report on their welfare. The officers work with local authorities and, depending on the circumstances, may personally search hotels, airports, hospitals, or even prisons. As they try to get the information, their first priority is Americans dead or injured.

Death

When an American dies abroad, the Bureau of Consular Affairs must locate and inform the next-of-kin. Sometimes discovering the next-of-kin is difficult. If the American's name is known, the Bureau's Office of Passport Services will search for his or her passport application. However, the information there may not be current.

The Bureau of Consular Affairs provides guidance to grieving family members on how to make arrangements for local burial or return of the remains to the U.S. The disposition of remains is affected by local laws, customs, and facilities, which are often vastly different from those in the U.S. The Bureau of Consular Affairs relays the family's instructions and necessary private funds to cover the costs involved to the embassy or consulate. The Department of State has no funds to assist in the return of remains or ashes of American citizens who die abroad. Upon completion of all formalities, the consular officer abroad prepares an official Foreign Service Report of Death, based upon the local death certificate, and sends it to the next-of-kin or legal representative for use in U.S. courts to settle estate matters.

A U.S. consular officer overseas has statutory responsibility for the personal estate of an American who dies abroad if the deceased has no legal representative in the country where the death occurred. The consular officer takes possession of personal effects, such as convertible assets, apparel, jewelry, personal documents, and papers. The officer prepares an inventory and then carries out instructions from members of the deceased's family concerning the effects. A final statement of the account is then sent to the next-of-kin. The Diplomatic Pouch cannot be used to ship personal items, including valuables, but legal documents and correspondence relating to the estate can be transmitted by pouch. In Washington, the Bureau of Consular Affairs gives next-of-kin guidance on procedures to follow in preparing Letters Testamentary, Letters of Administration, and Affidavits of Next-of-Kin as acceptable evidence of legal claim of an estate.

Injury

In the case of an injured American, the embassy or consulate abroad notifies the task force, which notifies family members in the U.S. The Bureau of Consular Affairs can assist in sending private funds to the injured American; frequently it collects information on the individual's prior medical history and forwards it to the embassy or consulate. When necessary, the State Department assists in arranging the return of the injured American to the U.S. commercially, with appropriate medical escort, via commercial air ambulance or, occasionally, by U.S. Air Force medical evacuation aircraft. The use of Air Force facilities for a medical evacuation is authorized only under certain stringent conditions, and when commercial evacuation is not possible. The full expense must be borne by the injured American or his family.

Evacuation

Sometimes commercial transportation entering and leaving a country is disrupted during a political upheaval or natural disaster. If this happens, and if it appears unsafe for Americans to remain, the embassy and consulates will work with the task force in Washington to charter special airflights and ground transportation to help Americans to depart. The U.S. Government cannot order Americans to leave a foreign country. It can only advise and try to assist those who wish to leave. By law, an American receiving evacuation assistance is required to sign a promissory note agreeing to reimburse the government for some of the evacuation costs.

More information can be found on the form itself, available at: http://foia.state.gov/Forms/Services/ds3072.pdf.

Privacy Act

The provisions of the Privacy Act are designed to protect the privacy and rights of Americans, but occasionally they complicate our efforts to assist citizens abroad. As a rule, consular officers may not reveal information regarding an individual Americans location, welfare, intentions, or problems to anyone, including family members and Congressional representatives, without the expressed consent of that individual. Although sympathetic to the distress this can cause concerned families, consular officers must comply with the provisions of the Privacy Act."

www.Travel.state.gov is packed with detailed information on how to handle emergencies in foreign locations. Familiarize yourself with the site before you travel. Use it for reference in an emergency or disaster event.

Chapter 15
Help: Where to Find It, How to Give It

Contact local authorities to inquire about help. If you need immediate assistance for life-threatening situations, dial 911 or your local emergency number. If the lines are busy use a radio or send a courier for help, then keep trying 911.

1.   Assistance

Throughout the disaster event and during the recovery phase it's important to monitor local radio and TV, newspapers, and other sources of information about where to get emergency housing, food and water, clothing, and financial assistance.

Direct assistance may come from many organizations, including the American Red Cross, the Salvation Army, and many civic and faith-based organizations. These organizations may provide food, shelter, counseling, and some monetary assistance, supplies, and may assist in clean up. Emergency food coupons may become available from the U.S. Department of Agriculture and state authorities.

In major disasters declared by the president, some federal assistance becomes available. This includes temporary housing, counseling, low interest loans and grants to cover damage not covered by victim's insurance policies. Note that the Federal grants will not have to be paid back, but they are limited and generally reserved for those who are not insured. Loans must be paid back, and will add to your overall financial burden on the property. Also, loans are restricted to the amount that your insurance doesn't cover. If you get one of these loans or grants, make sure you spend it on its intended purpose. If you don't, it's fraud. FEMA also has programs that help small businesses and farmers. FEMA's Mortgage and Rental Assistance Program is for eviction, foreclosure, and financial hardship cases caused by disasters. The Federal Assistance to Individuals and Households Program (IHP) offers grants for housing assistance and other critical needs. The Rental Assistance program can help if your home is unlivable after a disaster. The Minimal Repair Program is to help owners of homes with minor damage that are still livable. In addition, there may be money available to help with necessary expenses, including:

- Disaster-related medical and dental costs.
- Disaster-related funeral and burial costs.
- Clothing, household items, tools required for your job, and necessary educational materials.
- Fuels for primary heat sources.
- Clean up items.
- Disaster-related vehicle damage.
- Disaster-related moving and storage expenses.

Additional services that can be arranged through FEMA might include:

- Crisis counseling.
- Disaster Unemployment Assistance (DUA) if you're not eligible for regular unemployment insurance compensation.
- Legal services.
- Special tax considerations.

The Federal Emergency Management Agency (FEMA) will provide information through local media and community outreach about assistance and how to apply.

HUD offers Home Mortgage Insurance, which is basically a loan through approved lenders to rebuild or to buy another home. The Farm Service Agency may provide low interest disaster loans to farmers.

2.   Shelter & Housing Needs

See chapter 8, "Shelter and Evacuation," for information on community sheltering.

As explained above, if you lose your home and have nowhere to go for an extended period, your local, state, and federal emergency management people may have some housing assistance available:

- *Temporary housing* in the form of money to rent a place, or a government housing unit, which is typically a small mobile home or trailer.
- *Repair.* Money might be available in the form of loans or grants to repair damage that isn't covered by your own insurance, in order to make your home safe, sanitary, and functional.
- *Replacement.* There may be money to help with the cost of replacing a destroyed home not covered by the homeowner's insurance.
- *Permanent housing construction.* Help may be available in the form of direct assistance or money for construction, only in areas where no other type of housing assistance is available.

This all makes the situation look bright and rosy. Remember that you'll be competing with a lot of other people for these resources, and you must meet the qualifications for assistance.

See the contact information listed at the end of this chapter.

3.   How You Can Give Help

In most cases local authorities don't want or need hordes of undocumented and unorganized volunteers running around creating dangerous situations, security headaches, or logistical problems, or blocking access and causing confusion. Stay away from disaster scenes until volunteers are called for. If you want to be on the scene helping, join one of the many organizations that supply volunteers for that purpose. Many of them will train you, equip you, and provide transportation, and—very importantly—they can vouch for you and will know your background so you can be put to the most efficient use.

If you are needed at the disaster scene, bring your own food, water, and supplies so you're not putting an extra burden on an already overwhelmed supply.

Here are some U.S.-based organizations looking for reliable volunteers:

www.redcross.org—American Red Cross
www.salvationarmyusa.org—Salvation Army
www.usafreedomcorps.gov—USA Freedom Corps
www.medicalreservecorps.gov—Medical Reserve Corps
www.arrl.org—Amateur Radio Emergency Service
www.races.net—Radio Amateur Civil Emergency Service

www.nvoad.org—National Voluntary Organizations Active in Disaster *www.citizencorps.gov/programs/*—Community Emergency Response Team Program (CERT), Medical Reserve Corps, Fire Corps, USA onWatch, Volunteers in Police Service

Internationally there are dozens of organizations that can use dedicated volunteers. Visit http://www.reliefweb.int.

It's important to remember that volunteers need to be prepared mentally and physically for what's ahead of them. Volunteer disaster work is tedious, hazardous, unglamorous, frustrating, and emotionally draining.

In most cases, to be blunt and practical, money and blood are always two of the best things to donate. Non-perishable food donations are also good. Make those donations to organizations that are already recognized and organized enough to manage and distribute what you donate. Otherwise it might go to waste.

If you can't afford a monetary donation, and you can't go to the front lines to do relief work, donate some time working with local community organizations that help in troubled times. Religious and civic groups contribute enormously to relief efforts. Seriously consider helping by freeing up somebody else who might be needed at the disaster scene. Maybe you can cover their shift at work, watch the animals for a few days, babysit, house-sit . . . anything to help.

Appendix 1
Informational Resources

1.   Web-based

www.redcross.org—American Red Cross
www.salvationarmyusa.org—Salvation Army
www.usafreedomcorps.gov—USA Freedom Corps
www.medicalreservecorps.gov—Medical Reserve Corps
www.arrl.org—Amateur Radio Emergency Service (ARES)
www.races.net—Radio Amateur Civil Emergency Service (RACES)
www.nvoad.org—National Voluntary Organizations Active in Disaster
www.citizencorps.gov/programs/—Community Emergency Response Team Program (CERT), Medical Reserve Corps, Fire Corps, USAonWatch, Volunteers in Police Service
www.reliefweb.int—the U.N. Office for the Coordination of Humanitarian Affairs—Centers for Disease Control and Prevention
www.pandemicflu.gov—for pandemic flu information
http://.hhs.gov/emergency/—Department of Health and Human Services
http://disasterhelp/portaljhtml/index.jhtml—for assistance information
http://epa.gov—Environmental Protection Agency
www.fema.gov—Federal Emergency Management Agency
www.travel.state.gov—Department of State
www.nih.gov—National Institute of Health

www.fda.gov—Food and Drug Administration
www.doe.gov—Department of Energy
www.fbi.gov—Federal Bureau of Investigation

2.   And Some Phone Numbers . . .

Federal Emergency Management Agency: 1-800-621-3362 (621-FEMA)

Federal Citizen Information Center (FCIC): 1-800-333-4636 (FED-INFO)

American Red Cross National Headquarters: 1-866-438-4636 (GET-INFO)

Appendix 2
Simple Unknown Substance
Hazard Identification

In a large-scale disaster it may be hours or days before an emergency response unit can respond to a hazardous materials incident that isn't producing casualties. Some simple tests can provide you with some information about the hazards of unknown substances spilled or deposited in your community. It can also tell you if the substance might present a live germ hazard (e.g., a mysterious "white powder" event).

Even though material is not producing casualties you should evacuate the area for several hundred feet.

Be aware that these tests provide only basic information about the hazards of the substance. The tests are not comprehensive, and there is no test to determine if a substance is poison, unless you want to feed it to your pet rat, in which case the kids will hate you.

Take appropriate precautions and use personal protective equipment if you decide to handle any of the unknown material. You only need a small sample. Take notes on what you find and give them to the responders.

1. Physical Description and Air Reactivity

- What's the state of the material (solid, liquid, or gas)?
- What color is it?
- What consistency is it (for solids: powder, grains, chunk, etc.) and what viscosity (for liquids: like water, like oil, like cold molasses)?
- What clarity does it have (transparent, translucent, opaque)?

- Does it react when exposed to air (heat, smoke, gas, flame, etc.)? If so, it's **air reactive. Bad stuff**.

2.   Water Reactivity Test

- In a glass dish or test tube, carefully add a few drops of the unknown to a few drops of water. If there's heat, gas, or flame generated, it's **water reactive**. Don't try to wash it away.

3.   Water Solubility

- Does it dissolve in water? If not:
- Does it sink or float (is it less or more dense than water)?

4.   pH

- Test a liquid or a dissolved solution with pH paper. If it's less than 3 or greater than 12, it's highly **corrosive.** Note: "Germs" (biologic agents) will not survive in low or high pH (<5 or >9).

5.   Ignitability or Flammability

- Use a lighter or wooden match. Touch it to a few drops or small chunks of the unknown. If it lights, pull the lighter away. If it reacts violently, it's **explosive**. **Evacuate an appropriate area**. If it supports its own combustion, it's **flammable (a major fire hazard)**. If it goes out, hold the lighter to it for one second. If it burns, it's **combustible**.

6.   Oxidizer Test

- You'll need some weak hydrochloric acid and some starch-iodine paper for this test. Purchase the paper commercially or have the local chemistry teacher make it for you ahead of time. Wet a tiny piece of the paper with a drop or two of the acid. Then touch it to a drop or tiny piece of the unknown. If the paper turns dark purple or black, the unknown is an oxidizer. It can react with other substances and cause or accelerate a fire. Note: oxidizers kill "germs."

Note: At this point a sulfide test and a cyanide test are often done on unknowns with a pH greater than 10 to test for the presence of toxic hydrogen sulfide or cyanide. Don't bother. If the substance has a pH over 10, stay a large distance from it. A copper wire test in which a wire coated with some of the unknown is heated in a flame is also commonly performed to test for chlorides and halogens (indicated by a green flame).

So what has all this told you? You've determined if the substance is a fire or explosion hazard and if it's dangerously corrosive. Many corrosives are also respiratory hazards. You also know what will happen if you add water to the unknown in an attempt to dilute it or wash it way. And if the pH was high or low and/or it's an oxidizer, it's not likely that your unknown has any live germs in it. But you never know. Stay away from the stuff anyway until the professionals can test and dispose of it.

There are some problems with these tests. As mentioned before they don't tell you if a substance is poison. Some very potent acids will not show extreme pH on the strip, and some oxidizers cannot be identified with the starch-iodine paper. Germs may not survive in low or high pH or in oxidizers, but bio-toxins (e.g., ricin) might.

If nothing else, learning these tests will give you an awareness of the potential hazards of unknown substances.

Appendix 3
Rappelling/Lowering for High Rise Evacuation

Of the extreme high-rise evacuation methods mentioned in Chapter 15, it's the author's opinion that rappelling and lowering are the most practical means of getting yourself and others down in a "last resort" situation.

Assumptions:

1. Over two-thirds of high-rise fires start below the fifth floor.
2. Heat and sharps (glass and metal) are the primary threats to rope evac equipment. Regular nylon, polyester, and polypropylene climbing and rescue ropes may not be able to withstand the damage.
3. Smoke and operator error are the primary threats to rope evacuees.

Based on these assumptions, the following conclusions can be made:

1. Most high-rise rope evacs should only require 120 feet or less of rope (20 feet per floor plus 20 feet for anchoring). If the fire is above the 5th floor, the rope can be used to get evacuees to the floors below the fire, or a rope of appropriate length can be used to land evacuees on the ground (again, 20 feet per floor, plus 20 feet for anchoring).
2. a. Most nylon, polyester, and polypropylene ropes lose half their strength by the time they are exposed to temperatures of between

250 to 350 degrees. Testing has shown that some newer high-tensile fibers, Technora, for example, are two to three times as resistant to heat and significantly more resistant to abrasion than the fibers used in standard ropes.

b. Evacuate on the side least exposed to glass and metal sharps. This will be the side that's not in flames or that hasn't been blown out in the explosion. One of the advantages of simple rappel systems is that you can put your anchors anywhere.

3. a. Again, set your anchors on the side of the building that has the least amount of smoke exposure.

b. Because smoke, poisonous gases, and heat can cause you to disorient or pass out on rappel, do not use an "autoblock" backup (e.g., Grigri, Sum, autoblock knots) unless you are the last or only person using the rope to evacuate. Learn to rely on fireman's belays for backup. Fireman's belays are described later in the appendix.

c. There are two common operator errors that can ruin your day:

1. Misjudging the amount of friction you need to control the belay. The amount of friction you need increases as you get closer to the ground. Rappellers often find themselves going faster and faster, then losing control entirely.

2. Getting something caught in the rappel device. This will bring the evacuation to a screeching halt.

4. In order to prevent bad things from happening and to take advantage of the versatility and simplicity of rope evacuation systems, the author recommends taking rappelling courses from experienced, qualified trainers. In general, experienced canyoneers and

cavers know far more about the "ups and downs" of rappelling than the average climber or firefighter does. At a minimum your business or building security office should establish and train a "captain" for each floor. Even better, two captains for each floor. The captains should become an expert at anchoring and controlling the rope evacuations.

1. Basic Rope Evacuation Systems

There are three basic systems that can be used to evacuate:

	Pros	Cons
1. **Lowering systems** in which each evacuee is secured to the rope and lowered directly to the ground by somebody who controls the rope from above.	If there's enough time, everyone can get down, even if they don't have any rappelling experience. There's no chance of rappel devices becoming jammed. 2:1 lowering systems can be used to quickly lower evacuees and recover the rope without them having to de-rig.	If evacuee is injured or otherwise unable to remove himself from the tie-in, the entire system comes to a standstill.
2. **Rappel systems** in which each evacuee rigs the rope to a rappel brake on his or her harness and controls their own descent directly to the ground.		Requires prior rappelling experience. There will NOT be enough time to do a group rappelling class during an incident. A jammed rappel device will bring the entire system to a standstill.
3. **"Guided" rappels and lowers** in which the bottom end of the rope is anchored well away from the base of the building and evacuees are lowered or rappel along the guideline to a safe location.	Areas of heat, smoke, and dangerous debris can be avoided, and evacuees are landed in safe areas away from danger. Pros of rappelling or lowering apply.	Cons of rappelling or lowering apply.

Equipment For High-Rise Rope Evacuation

- **Rope.** Use static (low or no-stretch) canyoneering, caving, or rescue rope. Several companies (e.g., PMI and Bluewater) are producing static ropes with Technora and other high-tensile fibers. These are stronger, more abrasion resistant, and less susceptible to heat damage than standard fiber ropes. Ropes with a diameter of 9 to 13 mm (three-eighths to one-half-inch) are preferable if the drop can be kept under 120 feet. These fat diameters are easy to control. If the drop is going to be more than 120 feet, consider 8 mm or 9.2 mm ropes made with high-tensile fibers. 8 to 9.2 mm ropes do not give the control of fatter ropes, but they are considerably less bulky. You'll need at least 120 feet for simple lowers and rappels, 240 feet if you plan to use 2:1 lowering systems or to double the rope and rappel or lower on both strands simultaneously.

- **Rope Bag.** Rope bags are the best way to store and deploy a bag. Do not use rope-coiling techniques commonly used by climbers and firefighters. They are likely to tangle when you need them the most. A properly bagged rope can easily be anchored on one end and dropped, bag and all, directly to the ground without snarls or kinks.

- **Harness.** If you're going to be the only person using your rope evac system, get a good, simple climbing or canyoneering harness. If you plan to help others get down, you'll want to have a number of 12- to 14-foot slings made of one-inch tubular webbing. These slings are tied with a water knot and used as a "diaper seat" harness. Buy this webbing from a climbing store.

- **Carabiners.** These are strong snaplinks used to clip into the rope for various purposes. They come

Before tossing the bag over the edge, make sure the edge is padded. Remove anything that could get jammed in the rappel device (ties, necklaces) and tuck away long hair. If you're wearing heels, get into a pair of tennis shoes. Wear a helmet if one is available.

in various shapes and in locking and non-locking varieties. Locking varieties are by far more safe than non-locking when using them to secure an evacuee to a rope or rappel device, but people in panic mode seem to have a difficult time with locking carabiners. Also, when you've got 20 people to evacuate and 15 minutes to do it, the extra 10 seconds it takes to lock and unlock the 'biner each time can eat up a lot of seriously precious time. Use your discretion. Try keeping at least three lockers and three non-lockers in your kit.

- **Rappel/Lowering Device.** The author recommends a simple rappel device, like an ATC made by Black Diamond Equipment or an SBG II from Omega, that can be used to rappel or control a lower and that is easy to vary friction on. Avoid spring-loaded

A diaper harness made from 14 feet of webbing. An expedient method of rigging a "diaper seat" harness using a 14-foot piece of one-inch tubular webbing. Tie the ends together with a *water knot* (aka ring bend, left. The wings are brought up through the loop pulled up from between the legs, center. Attach the carabiner and rappel device to the wings, right. Snug up the harness and don't let it loosen and fall off the waist and down the thighs.

devices that will automatically lock you to the rope if you pass out and let go.

- **Anchor Material.** The rope can be tied directly into the anchor, or clipped into an anchor sling with a carabiner. Use one of your 12-foot tubular webbings, or keep a 15-foot piece of Omni-sling in your kit specifically for anchors.

- **Helmet and Gloves.** If a helmet is available, wear it. But don't waste time ferrying a single helmet up and down between evacuees. Gloves are not necessary if you know how to rappel and control your friction device. Gloves are often used by inexperienced rappellers. While a glove can protect the hand from rope burns, it's difficult to grip the rope correctly with a glove, and wearing gloves can ultimately result in less control. If you use gloves, make sure they are soft and ergonomic—pre-curved to the shape of a semi-clenched hand.

Techniques

Anchors

Escape anchors are probably going to be one of two types. They might be **wrapped** around a stout structure or **jammed** in a choke-point. For an entertaining primer on structural anchors, watch the classic Eastwood-Burton war movie *Where Eagles Dare.*

Anchor Basics

- Make sure the anchor is solid against the direction of pull (usually the fall-line).
- Pad the anchor and the rope against broken glass and abrasion.

Lowering Technique

Before sending each evacuee down, make sure they understand that when they reach the ground they are to step out of the harness without disconnecting the carabiner so the belayer can retrieve rope, 'biner, and harness. Here are two methods of lowering:

1.   Clip a carabiner into the end of a rope (figure 8 knot) and to the diaper seat of an evacuee. Set the rappel device on an anchor as indicated on its decals or owner's manual. Send the evacuee off and control the rate of descent. Having a "spotter" on the edge to watch the evacuee and relay instructions will make the operation smoother.

2.   Use a 2:1 lowering system (doubled rope through the evacuee's carabiner). One end of the rope is tied to the anchor, the other controlled by the belayer. The advantage of this system is that if anything goes wrong, the rope can be pulled through the evacuee's carabiner and retrieved.

By doubling the rope and securing the middle to the anchor, two 2:1 lowering systems can be operated at the same time. This is a fast, efficient way of getting people to safety.

Rappelling Technique

Contrary to the way it looks in the movies, rappelling is seriously complicated in terms of the various methods and devices used to descend and the physics and dynamics of the procedure. Don't try anything heroic or stupid. Upside-down-and-backward and bounding commando rappels are ridiculous and excessively dangerous.

Fig. A, A runner knot jammed behind a snugly closed door on the hinged side, opposite the latch.

Fig. B, A runner girth hitched around a stout chair leg and blocked by the same door.

Fig. C, A runner girth hitched around a heavy sofa.

Fig. D, A rappel rope tied directly to a structural feature.

Anchors are everywhere.

Here's the basic procedure:

1. Attach the end of the rope to the anchor and drop the other end to the ground, the next roof, or alongside a target ledge or balcony.

2. Attach the rope to your rappel device and your rappel device to your harness according to the manufacturers' instructions. If you're using locking carabiners, lock them. Remember when you're rigging your device that you will be sliding faster as you get closer to the ground. It's critical that you have lots of friction in your device at the top so there will be enough friction to control the descent closer to the ground.

3. Quickly secure anything loose that could jam in the rappel device. Remove necklaces and chains, tuck away hair, button sleeves, tuck in shirt-tails. This is important. If you screw up and jam your device, you will die hanging on the rope and no one above you will be able to use the rope for rappelling.

4. Grab the rope with your "guide" hand about a foot above the rappel device. Use this for support and balance only, but not to control the rappel.

5. Grab the rope with your brake hand just below the rappel device and slide the hand back and wrap the rope across the hip. From this point, do not remove your brake hand from the rope until you have reached your destination safely.

6. Sit on the edge of the building, balcony, or window ledge and ooze carefully but quickly over.

7. Face the wall and put both feet on the wall, shoulder-width apart, then lean back and let out a few inches of rope until you're in the proper position.

8. Rappel down by carefully but smoothly letting the rope in your brake hand slide through the rappel device, walking backward down the wall.

9. Stay leaning out as pictured, while rappelling. Leaning in can cause items to get caught and jam the rappel device. Leaning out keeps the rope farther away from sharp edges, shattered glass, and items that might have absorbed radiated heat. It also keeps more of the foot sole on the wall and prevents slipping. Leaning too far back can cause you to tip upside down.

10. If you are dangling from overhanging eaves, just sit comfortably upright in the harness and rappel smoothly.

11. Stay in the fall-line directly below your anchor. Moving too far to either side of the fall-line can cause you to tip over, swing, or severely damage the rope.

12. When you are safely on the ground or at your target location, release the rope from your rappel device, then look upward and yell "OFF RAPPEL!" as loudly as possible to anyone above who is waiting to get on the rope. Chances are there will be too much noise for anyone to hear voices and too much smoke to see, so use your FRS radios or pre-arrange some rope signals beforehand (e.g., two very hard tugs for "off rappel").

Fireman's Belay

If you're in a group of people who plan to rappel, send someone down first who is a competent rappeller and who knows how to do a fireman's belay. With a fireman's belay the belayer can stop the fall of a rappeller who lets go of the rope for any reason.

To perform a fireman's belay:

A climber showing the proper body position for rappelling
on a wall.

- The belayer takes cover behind whatever cover he/she can find, out of the direct fall-line, that shields him/her from falling debris but allows an unobstructed view of the rappeller.
- The belayer holds the rope loosely while the rappeller descends. There must be enough slack in the rope at the bottom so the belay does not interfere with the rope moving through the rappel device.
- If the rappeller loses control, the belayer pulls down and back to tighten the rope, which applies friction at the rappel device and stops the fall.
- The belayer can hold the rappeller securely in position until the rappeller regains control, or lower the rappeller by varying the tension on the rope.

A climber using a Fireman's Belay. By pulling down on
the rope she can stop or slow the rappeller above.

Guided Systems

A guided system directs a rappeller or a lowered victim to a particular landing spot away from the fall-line, smoke, sharps, and heat. The first person down simply rappels or is lowered to the ground and then pulls the rope away from the building to the preferred site. Then he/she pulls tightly to remove the slack and anchors the rope to a stout anchor. In an urban situation this bottom anchor will be anything that won't move: a tree, a truck, a column. When the bottom anchor is secure, each person in turn attaches the "cows tails" of their harness to the guideline and they are lowered along the guideline with a second line (usually the other half of the rappel rope). Or, each person can rappel along the guideline using the second rope in their rappel device. Whichever method is employed, when the person reaches the bottom he/she must unclip from the guide rope and step out of the harness without unclipping the carabiner from the second line, so the harness, carabiner, and rope can all be pulled back up for the next person.

Adjusting Friction

Probably the two easiest ways for a layman to add additional friction to his device during a rappel are:

1. Pass the rope around the back to the opposite hand.

2. Before starting the rappel, put an additional carabiner to the leg loop on the brake-hand side, and when the time is right pass the rope through that carabiner. Note that this will then require the rappel to be controlled out front rather than back at the hip.

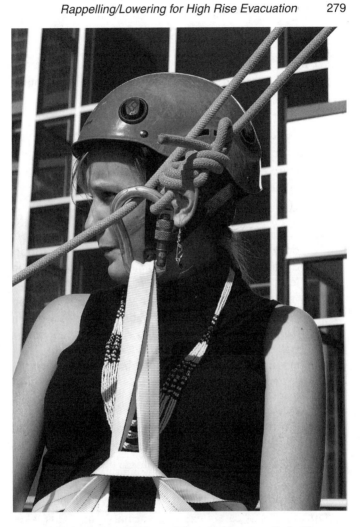

Rigging for a guided lower. Lowers can be controlled with the friction of the lowering rope through a rappel/belay device attached to an anchor, or from wrapping the rope around a structurally-sound feature such as a solid rail, a stair frame, or column.

Contingencies for Screw-Ups

Other than not knowing *how* to rappel, the most common problem encountered will be getting something jammed in the rappel/belay device. A third problem will be the tendency for a rappeller to freeze up while attempting to pass hazardous sections of the rappel. Having an extra rappel device for a contingency anchor can prevent the tragic failure of the rappel system due to someone getting jammed or stranded on the rope.

A contingency anchor is rigged as follows:

1. The middle of the rope is attached to the extra rappel device and the device is then attached to the rappel anchor sling in the same manner it would be attached to your harness if you were rappelling with it.
2. A loop of the "brake" side of the rope is pulled through the carabiner and then brought forward in front of the device and a slip knot is applied across both strands. Further secure the slip knot by tying the end of the loop in an overhand knot around the strands.

If the rappeller gets jammed or stops for some unknown reason, the overhand and slip knots can be released and the rope controlled through the rappel device to lower the rappeller to the ground. The ability to do this is increasingly important as more smoke and heat pervade the fall-line.

There are other methods of setting up contingency systems with just carabiners and special knots. This takes training and competence to set up correctly and efficiently.

One excellent source of this type of training—easily modified to urban rappels—is the American Canyoneering Association (*www.canyoneering.net*).

Appendix 4
An Improvised Level C Exposure Suit

Protective clothing for hazardous materials operations provides varying levels of protection from chemical and biological agents, radiation exposure, and extremes of temperature. Level A is the highest level of protection and uses a fully encapsulating chemical-resistant suit with a self-contained breathing apparatus (SCBA) inside the suit. Level B also uses a chemical resistant one-piece suit which may or may not be totally encapsulating, and an SCBA that may be inside or outside the suit. If the suit is not totally encapsulating, the sleeves and cuffs are usually taped to the gloves and booties to make a seal and minimize chem/bio/rad penetration. Level C includes a one or two piece chemically resistant suit and an APR (air purifying respirator, aka "gas mask"). Level D usually consists of a simple coverall and general safety gear (goggles, gloves, etc.).

Commercial hazmat suits are expensive and bulky. In the worst case scenario, and only when you are truly convinced that you cannot safely evacuate or shelter in place, and your life depends on it, you can improvise protective clothing approaching the C level from the following equipment:

- Gas mask, or even a quality smoke hood (available from a safety supply store).
- Rain pant and hooded top that are completely waterproof, preferably made of heavy-duty vinyl or a rubberized fabric that will not absorb liquids. A cheap vinyl rain suit is well suited for this purpose.

Do not use breathable fabrics. Non-breathable and un-vented is best.

- Dishwashing gloves
- Rain overboots ("galoshes") or plastic trash bags
- Duct tape

Notice that all of these items are on the list of items recommended for a comprehensive disaster supply kit. Here's the sequence for "suiting-up":

1. If exposure is in progress in close proximity, hold your breath and place a new filter on the mask. If this procedure is going to take longer than you can hold your breath, immediately cover your mouth and nose with a surgical mask or soft material (e.g., pull your T-shirt collar up over your face).

2. Put on your mask or your smoke hood. We'll assume here you have preplanned this, and that your mask is the right size and the straps are loosened. Follow the instructions that came with the mask or hood. The general procedure for donning a mask is as follows:

   a. With the headstraps pulled back, put your chin in its place in the mask and pull the mask onto the face and the straps over the head. Tighten the straps as directed.

   b. Exhale, then cover the PAPR air tube connector or the APR air intake on the filter with a hand and keep it there for a few seconds. Breathe in. The mask should make an obvious vacuum seal on the face, and the vacuum should remain while you keep your hand over the intake. If the vacuum releases, the seal is bad. Reposition the mask and retighten the straps, then check the seal again. If you're using a PAPR (powered or positive pressure air purifying respirator), connect the air tube and turn the unit on.

3. Pull on the shell pants and don the jacket and zip it fully closed. Pull the hood up over the mask and tighten the hood closure.

4. Pull on the galoshes or pull two garbage bags over each foot (leave your shoes on).

5. Duct tape the juncture of your pants cuffs and the galoshes or garbage bag. Run a strip of duct tape around the foot to secure the bag tightly close to the foot.

6. Tape the hem of the coat to the waist of the pants, and the edge of the hood to the mask (but only if the hood is big enough to prevent the mask from pulling away from the face when the head is turned).

7. Put on gloves.

8. Tape the gloves to the cuff of the sleeve.

How long can this suit be relied on? It depends on what it's made of and what kind of exposure is occurring. The function of this suit is to get you out of an exposure hazard that cannot be handled by shelter in place. It's going to provide a modicum of protection for a limited amount of time—minutes, not hours. Remember that this suit provides only temporary protection from chemicals, biologicals, and ingestion or inhalation of radioactive particles. It does not provide significant protection from heat extremes. It is sweaty, unventilated, and uncomfortable. Remember the following points:

- Get out and get away. Don't hang around, expecting your suit to protect you for hours.

- If you truly needed this suit, you will need to be properly decontaminated and everything you wear will need to be handled properly to prevent secondary exposures.

- Anything you carry with you will also need to be protected—covered by plastic garbage bags and sealed. These will also need to be decontaminated properly.

- If you don't have this gear, don't panic. Some protection is better than none. During brief exposures—and most exposures are going to be brief—normal clothing and some form of face protection (anything ranging from an N95 mask and swim goggles to a scarf over the face,) may provide enough protection to make the difference between being sick and being dead. As soon as the exposure has ended, remove clothing, decontaminate, and seek medical advice.

Appendix 5
Potty Matters

In an emergency during which sewage systems are not functioning, it will be necessary to create emergency toilets. The other option is to have everyone running around, pooping at any random location that suits his or her fancy. It's messy, smelly, and very unhealthy. Latrines and toilets are needed to allow for safe collection and handling of human waste.

Here are the basics of emergency toilets and latrines:

- Provide some privacy if possible, using barriers (walls) or any sort. Most of the population will not use a latrine that's in open view.

- Locate toilets and latrines away from food preparation or eating areas.

- Locate toilets and latrines at least 100 feet away from bodies of surface water (lakes, rivers, etc.), and at least 100 feet downhill or downstream from drinking water resources and inhabitations.

- If possible, provide running water, soap, paper towels, and a garbage container next to the toilet(s). If that's not possible, make hand sanitizer available. Encourage (by whatever means) hand washing or sanitizing to prevent the spread of severe gastrointestinal diseases.

- If the toilet or latrine has a door or covers of any sort, keep them closed when not in use to minimize insects, animals, and stench.

- In an urban disaster setting, use the following hierarchy of toilets: functioning flush toilets; personal porta-potties or public portable toilets; emergency bucket/bowl toilets and garbage bags; hole and pit latrines.

Making an Emergency Toilet from a Flush Toilet or Bucket

- Line the inside of a five-gallon bucket or toilet bowl with two heavy-duty plastic garbage bags.
- Once daily add a cup of 1:10 bleach (3–6 percent sodium hypochlorite) and water to control pathogens and odor. Or, put a cup or two of kitty litter, ashes, sawdust, or sand into the bags. If you have a limited amount of kitty litter, mix with a filler like ashes, sand, or sawdust first.
- At the end of the day, seal the bags and store them in a protected area, out of the sun, where animals and insects will not disturb them and smell will not pervade living and dining areas.
- Listen to area media and speak with health or sanitation department officials for instructions on what to do with the stored waste.

Latrines

A latrine is basically a hole that's dug to collect human waste. These can range from "catholes" (a simple one-use hole) to large pit and trench latrines for public use. Since it's difficult to know where the hard pan or water table is without digging into it, latrines are not appropriate for urban locations that will continue to be areas of inhabitation or commerce. The carry-over hygiene problems will be unpleasant.

Here are the latrine basics:

- Public-use latrines should be at least three feet deep but at least one foot above the hard pan or the water table.
- After each use, the "doodie" should be covered with dirt, lime, or ash to keep the odor down and to minimize infestation by insects and animals.
- Consider covering the latrine with a piece of scrap board between uses.

The Web is full of sites that can give you the poop on latrine science. Get on your browser and type in "latrine."

Appendix 6
Simple Self Defense

If you find yourself in a situation where you have that feeling that you are at risk of attack, stay attentive and aware of your surroundings. Here are some suggestions:

- Keep your eyes alternately on the hands and eyes of anyone nearby. If someone catches you looking and quickly looks away or hides the hands, be suspicious and take another path.
- Cross the street or go around the block to avoid suspicious groups.
- Avoid speaking to anyone, and when you do speak make certain you don't say anything that could be misinterpreted as insulting, inflammatory, or threatening.

If someone produces a weapon and threatens you, you really only have three choices: 1) Do what they tell you to do. 2) Run like hell. 3) Fight and be injured, possibly killed. When no weapon is involved, you have more options.

Once a weaponless act of violence has begun, be prepared to defend yourself to minimize the damage.

- Make noise and yell for help.
- Put your hands in front of your face, with the forearms and elbows drawn in to protect your neck, chest, and upper abdomen. Tuck your chin in. Close your mouth tightly and clench your teeth to prevent broken teeth and a busted jawbone.
- Circle away and to the opposite side of the dominant hand and foot of an attacker. A fighter will usually

stand with the dominant hand pulled back, ready to strike, and the dominant foot slightly behind the other. If he swings with the dominant hand, pull back and lean or move to one side or another. The non-dominant hand will likely be used to threaten and distract you from blocking the real power punch that will be coming from his dominant hand or foot.

- Stay as far away from the attacker as possible. Get something in between you and your attackers—a parked car, a pile of garbage. If your attacker gets your back against a wall and closes in, step in next to him and wrap your arms around him to keep him from landing heavy blows.

Aggression can be an effective means of defense, but should be a last resort since it's likely to anger your attackers even more. Sometimes an aggressive move will distract an attacker and allow a quick escape.

- Beforehand get some coaching from a martial arts expert on how to properly kick and strike without injuring yourself or losing your balance.
- Use a foot, elbow, or knee to the groin, abdomen, face, or throat. Gouge eyes. If it looks grim, grab and use any weapon at hand.
- If you get knocked to the ground and can't get up quickly, get onto your side in a tight fetal position. Protect your head, neck, and face with your arms and hands, and your internal organs with tightly drawn-up knees.

Here's another bit of honesty that will ruin some of your vigilante fantasies: becoming a kung fu expert is not going to make you invincible. In fact, a black belt pitted against a professional boxer will almost always end up on the sharp end of the stick. Why? Because as soon as your enemy does something you haven't seen in the dojo, you've lost the advantage and the match then goes to the meanest. This isn't to say you shouldn't take karate. It does mean that you should include a wide range of weapon-based and weaponless fighting forms in your training if you intend to be serious about defending yourself against street fighters or groups of enraged pitchfork-wielding campesinos.

> "Perfect wisdom is unplanned. Perfect living offers no guarantee of a peaceful death."
> —Master Po, from the TV series *Kung Fu*

Appendix 7
Go-Kits

What you decide to include in your Go-Kit is going to depend on how much money you have to spend, how spoiled you are, and how much you're willing to lug all that weight around with you. The best personal kit is the one you're willing to carry around. For most people, that means something small.

The charts on the following pages make suggestions for kit items based on the intended scope of the kit and the level of needs (the Tier) that you want it to cater to. This is all open to opinion and no two people will consider the same items essential or non-essential.

Note that we haven't addressed office kits here. An adequate office kit will be similar to a comprehensive Tier 1 and 2 Individual or Home Kit, with the possible addition of specialty items related to escape systems (e.g., rope, etc.) and work-specific emergency tasks (see chapter 12).

Individual Kit
Take along to the office and to supplement home and vehicle kits
Basic
Tier 1 - Simple Survival (essential)

- ☐ Container (hip or fanny pack or quality hydration pack)*
- ☐ 1 quarts (liter) fluid per day
- ☐ Non-perishable equivalent of 3 meals per day
- ☐ cold climate items
- ☐ construction-strength garbage bags, 2
- ☐ N95 Mask

Tier 2 - Safety/Security (recommended)

- ☐ Communications: radio and cell phone **** and extra batteries or means of charging.
- ☐ Communications/contacts list
- ☐ LED headlamp and extra batteries
- ☐ Small first aid kit
- ☐ Change of clothes
- ☐ multi-tool
- ☐ Basic hygiene items (handwipes, toothbrush, soap, toothpaste, toilet paper, etc.)
- ☐ $25-100 per day
- ☐ important documents, including duplicates/copies of important IDs
- ☐ Matches/lighter protected in double ziplock bags
- ☐ whistle
- ☐ prescription meds
- ☐ additional water (up to 1 gallon per day)
- ☐ work gloves

Tier 3 - Comfort/Convenience (non-essential)

- ☐ Extensive hygiene items (towels, shampoo, etc.)

Comprehensive
Tier 1 - Simple Survival (essential)

- ☐ Water filter

Tier 2 - Safety/Security (recommended)

- ☐ Helmet (any helmet is better than no helmet when doing search and rescue)
- ☐ Smoke hood
- ☐ Extra protective clothing (for the equivalent of a makeshift Class C hazard suit).
- ☐ EMT shears
- ☐ Gas mask (air purifying respirator)
- ☐ Extra prescription glasses or contact lenses

Automobile Kit

Basic

Tier 1 - Simple Survival (essential)

- [ ] Container (heavy duty duffle or gym bag, or large ammo case or sealable buckle)
- [ ] 1 gallon water per person normally in car
- [ ] Equivalent of 3 meals per day per person normally in the car

Tier 2 - Safety/Security (recommended)

- [ ] Jumper cables
- [ ] Bright caution tape or surveyor's tape
- [ ] Traction aids: sand or cat litter; sand ladders, carpet mats, etc
- [ ] Tire sealant and/or tubeless tire repair kit
- [ ] Extra clothing
- [ ] Extra blankets, sleeping bags
- [ ] Flashlight and extra batteries
- [ ] Ice scraper and brush
- [ ] Road flares or emergency strobes (with Krypton or high-intensity LED bulbs)
- [ ] Tow chain or cable

Tier 3 - Comfort/Convenience (non-essential)

- [ ] Rags, paper towels
- [ ] Wrenches, screwdrivers

Comprehensive

Tier 3 - Comfort/Convenience (non-essential)

- [ ] Air compressor
- [ ] 12-volt jump start pack or battery boost
- [ ] solar-powered 12-volt trickle battery charger

Home Kit
Basic
Tier 1 - Simple Survival (essential)

- ☐ Non-perishable food for 3 days per person (or equivalent of three meals per person per day)
- ☐ Large construction-strength plastic bags, 2 per person (for emergency shelter and hygiene)
- ☐ Container (backpack*)
- ☐ Water, 1 gallon per day per person**

Tier 2 - Safety/Security (recommended)

- ☐ Multi-tool
- ☐ Wrench (for valve shut-off)
- ☐ Coffee filter for water filtering
- ☐ Toilet paper, 1 roll per day per 3 persons
- ☐ Bleach (sodium hypochlorite 3-6%), 1 pint
- ☐ LED headlamp, 1 per person, with extra batteries.***
- ☐ Communications: Radio and cell phone ****
- ☐ Communications /contact list
- ☐ Group or family first aid kit*****
- ☐ One entire change of clothing per person
- ☐ Sanitation and hygiene items
- ☐ Matches and/or lighter (protected in a ziplock bag)
- ☐ Whistle
- ☐ $25 cash per person per day
- ☐ prescription medications
- ☐ important documents
- ☐ essential pet items
- ☐ fire extinguisher
- ☐ work gloves
- ☐ duct tape
- ☐ essential geriatrics items

Tier 3 - Comfort/Convenience (non-essential)

- ☐ mirror
- ☐ writing kit (paper, pencils, pens, etc)
- ☐ cord, rope
- ☐ aluminum foil, plastic wrap
- ☐ games, cards, books
- ☐ sugar, salt, pepper

Home Kit
Comprehensive
Tier 1 - Simple Survival (essential)

- ☐ Cook-stove and fuel
- ☐ Water filter; water purification tablets
- ☐ Cooking utensils
- ☐ tent

Tier 2 - Safety/Security (recommended)

- ☐ sleeping pads
- ☐ camp shovel
- ☐ dish soap
- ☐ clothing detergent
- ☐ plastic sheeting or tarps (for sealing rooms during shelter in place)
- ☐ Backcountry survival kit
- ☐ extra 1-5 gallon containers for water and hygiene (carrying water, latrine buckets, dish- and clothes-washing containers)
- ☐ Fire escape ladder (foldable)
- ☐ crow bar
- ☐ radiation monitor
- ☐ N95 mask per person^
- ☐ Swim goggles or swim glasses^

Tier 3 - Comfort/Convenience (non-essential)

- ☐ Bailing wire (repairs)
- ☐ Hauling/pulling rig
- ☐ Pliers
- ☐ Axe or hatchet
- ☐ Gas chainsaw and fuel
- ☐ Generator and fuel
- ☐ Solar chargers
- ☐ Raft or inflatable kayak (got paddles?)

---

* For portability a quality backpack is recommended. Get it at a climbing shop. Climber's, canyoneer's, or caver's bags are built to withstand serious abuse and heavy loads. Use military surplus bags ONLY if they're modern and in good shape. If you load up with Tier 2 and 3 items, you're going to need expedition-capacity bags.

** Or equivalent in a combination of water and other fl uids (juices, etc.). If this seems excessive, remember that water will be needed for drinking, cooking, and hygiene.

*** With today's plastic enclosed LED lights so readily available, there is little reason to use metal flashlights that can collect a static charge and pose a spark hazard. It will help if all your battery-powered appliances use the same size battery. Include a bulk-pack of disposable batteries in your kit or multiple sets of rechargeable batteries and a solar charger if a generator or inverter are not available.

**** A good handheld ham tri-band (HF/VHF/UHF) radio will provide multi-band emergency transceiver capabilities, including FRS, GMRS, MURS, and CB frequencies. They will scan all frequencies from HF to high UHF, including NOAA and public safety bands, eliminating the need for a separate scanner. Ham radios do require licensing to transmit on, but not to own.

***** Don't forget to include sunscreen and mosquito repellent in your group first aid kit.

^ Inferior but helpful substitute for a full face mask (APR).